FINTECH POLICY TOOL KIT FOR REGULATORS AND POLICY MAKERS IN ASIA AND THE PACIFIC

MARCH 2022

ASIAN DEVELOPMENT BANK

Creative Commons Attribution 3.0 IGO license (CC BY 3.0 IGO)

ISBN 978-92-9269-367-1 (print); 978-92-9269-368-8 (electronic); 978-92-9269-369-5 (ebook)
Publication Stock No. TIM220043-2
DOI: http://dx.doi.org/10.22617/TIM20043-2

Notes:
In this publication, "$" refers to the United States dollar (unless otherwise stated), "W" refers to the won.

ADB recognizes "China" as the People's Republic of China; "Hong Kong" as Hong Kong, China; "Korea" as the Republic of Korea; "Laos" as the Lao People's Democratic Republic; and "Vietnam" as Viet Nam.

Cover design by Keisuke Taketani.

CONTENTS

TABLE, FIGURES, AND BOXES

TABLE

FIGURES

BOXES

FOREWORD

Twenty years ago, the world's first mobile money service was launched in the Philippines, a harbinger of the promise that financial technologies would hold for developing countries globally.

Since then, digital financial services have burgeoned from simple peer-to-peer money transfers to cutting-edge fintech that employs the latest technologies in distributed ledgers, digital banking, and central bank digital currencies.

More importantly, such fintech development is allowing us to broaden financial inclusion. Fintech increases financial access and delivers new products and services—especially to the unbanked and underserved in rural areas. In 2019, investment in fintech across Asia and the Pacific from venture capital and private equity firms was a hefty $13 billion—and this in an industry that remains at a relatively early stage of development.

The Asian Development Bank (ADB) has developed the Fintech Policy Tool Kit to help regulators and policy makers in Asia and the Pacific get the most out of the emerging technologies, a task made even more urgent by the challenges of the coronavirus disease (COVID-19) pandemic.

The dramatic restrictions on movement caused by the pandemic outbreak have underscored just how quickly new technology can be adopted and adapted to provide virtual ways of working and living. The pandemic has amplified the need to further digitize the financial sector and expand online banking and digital payment systems.

Through their innovations, fintech firms are helping to ensure business and government continuity at a crucial time. Indeed, even though many of these firms have not escaped the major economic distress caused by COVID-19, they are already creatively adjusting products and services to meet the needs of users struggling with the impact of the pandemic. This is bringing significant benefits to consumers and investors.

ADB has been actively involved in fintech over the years and has learned much from fintech projects we have piloted in Georgia, Papua New Guinea, the Philippines, and others. These pilot projects are helping transform organizations and cultures, driving coordination across government agencies and allowing individuals to better understand and absorb the new capabilities the technologies offer. They are allowing us to identify just how fintech can best accelerate financial inclusion and inclusive growth.

However, the increased adaptation and speed of fintech developments carry substantial risks that call for regulators and policy makers to balance the promotion of innovation and invention, financial stability, and customer protection. This is essential if innovators, investors, and consumers are to feel safe and build trust.

To apply appropriate safeguards and mitigate risks, regulators and policy makers must therefore understand, monitor, and supervise the fast-evolving, technology-driven developments. Appropriate tools and solutions—including new technologies such as regtech and suptech for managing regulatory processes and supporting supervision—will greatly help.

The emerging technological innovations will be at the heart of fintech development—staying with us for years to come. Through proactive consideration of new regulations and adaptation of existing regulations and policies, we can ensure that the benefits of these products are enriching, sustainable, and available to everyone.

As we collectively navigate this process, therefore, the continued support and engagement of each stakeholder is critical. The Fintech Policy Tool Kit aims to help citizens, businesses, and governments realize an inclusive fintech ecosystem for robust economic growth, greater equality, and lower poverty during these challenging times.

 I am grateful to the authors, researchers, and editors of the tool kit for their contributions to this important knowledge product.

Bruno Carrasco
Director General concurrently Chief Compliance Officer,
Sustainable Development and Climate Change Department
Asian Development Bank

ACKNOWLEDGMENTS

The *Fintech Policy Tool Kit for Regulators and Policy Makers in Asia and the Pacific* is a product of the Sustainable Development and Climate Change Department (SDCC) of the Asian Development Bank (ADB). This tool kit was prepared as part of ADB's support to knowledge work on digital financial services among its developing member countries.

The tool kit was financed by ADB's knowledge and support technical assistance 9364: Strengthening Financial Sector Operations in Asia and the Pacific which is financed on a grant basis by ADB's Technical Assistance Special Fund, Financial Sector Development Partnership Special Fund,[1] High-Level Technology Fund,[2] and the Republic of Korea e-Asia and Knowledge Partnership Fund.[3]

Junkyu Lee, Chief of Finance Sector Group, headed a core team of staff in preparing the tool kit. Sung Su Kim, financial specialist (Inclusive Finance), coordinated and contributed to the production of the publication with technical inputs provided by John Owens (consultant).

Technical and research support was provided by Arup Chatterjee, Lisette Cipriano, Hyungchan Lee, Jae Deuk Lee, Peter Rosenkranz, Duong T. Nguyen, Katherine Mitzi Co, Raquel Borres, and Laila Catherina Deles. Additional research support was provided by Alyssa Villanueva and Mikko Marl Diaz.

The team wishes to thank policy makers, financial regulators, academia, and representatives from development partners who participated and presented at workshops held on 21–22 July 2020 and 28–29 September 2020, and made suggestions for developing the report.

The team greatly appreciates staff in ADB headquarters and in resident missions who contributed to the knowledge events, particularly ADB Vice-President for Knowledge Management and Sustainable Development Bambang Susantono and SDCC Director General Bruno Carrasco for their proactive support in the realization of the knowledge events and the report.

The team would like to express a special gratitude to Woochong Um, managing director general in ADB, who kindly delivered opening remarks and played a moderator role in the Asian Fintech Policy Roundtable Meeting on 28th September 2020.

We thank all contributors for their generous support of this publication despite the difficult situation caused by the coronavirus disease.

Finally, the team also acknowledges colleagues from the Department of Communications for their continuous support in disseminating the report.

---

[1] Established by ADB. Financing partner: the Government of Luxembourg.
[2] Administered by ADB. Financing partner: the Government of Japan.
[3] Administered by ADB.

ABBREVIATIONS

ADB	Asian Development Bank
AFPI	Indonesian Fintech Lenders Association
AI	artificial intelligence
API	application programming interface
ASEAN	Association of Southeast Asian Nations
BIS	Bank for International Settlements
BSP	Bangko Sentral ng Pilipinas
COVID-19	coronavirus disease
DLT	distributed ledger technology
EU	European Union
FATF	Financial Action Task Force
GDPR	General Data Protection Regulation
ID	identification
IOT	Internet of Things
ISO	International Organization for Standardization
IT	information technology
KYC	know-your-customer
MAS	Monetary Authority of Singapore
OJK	Otoritas Jasa Keuangan/Financial Services Authority
P2P	peer-to-peer
POS	point-of-sale
PRC	People's Republic of China
QR	quick response
SDGs	Sustainable Development Goals
SMEs	small and medium-sized enterprises
UK	United Kingdom
US	United States

KEY CONTENT

This tool kit aims to help policy makers:

1 Understand the level of development of financial technologies in each market.

2 Learn from the experiences of others in the region and avoid reinventing the wheel.

3 Ensure an appropriate legal and regulatory framework that provides a clear mandate for the financial regulator to license and provide adequate oversight over new financial technologies and players.

4 Ensure the financial regulator has adequate capacity in trained staff and tools such as regulatory and supervisory technologies.

5 Understand the role and level of foundational infrastructure, specifically identification, payment, and data-sharing infrastructure.

6 Follow latest developments that promote use of fintech-enabled financial services, including understanding the three main regulatory approaches.

7 Know the key aspects of prudential and market conduct regulatory approaches for digital finance.

8 Support digital financial awareness and literacy.

9 Support competition, inter-regulatory coordination, and public–private dialogue.

10 Ensure a balanced focus on digital financial consumer protection issues in the digital age, especially as they relate to cybersecurity, data privacy, and protection.

Let's get started.

Fintech Policy Tool Kit

For Regulators and Policy Makers in Asia and the Pacific

DEVELOPING REGULATORY AND SUPERVISORY CAPACITY

Challenge | Regulators and supervisors must balance financial integrity, consumer protection, and financial stability— their primary goals— with an environment that enables the innovation crucial to fintech.

Core principles | The Bank for International Settlements (BIS) consultative document lays down core principles for creating an enabling environment and ensuring effective oversight and supervision of fintech

POLICY ENVIRONMENT AND FISCAL INCENTIVES

Government policies and fiscal incentives can play a key role, especially in attracting entrepreneurs and investors, and providing incentives to support fintech start-ups and promote adoption of fintech services.

3 FOUNDATIONAL INFRASTRUCTURAL ISSUES

 identification infrastructure

 payment infrastructure

 data-sharing infrastructure

ENSURING RESPONSIBLE FINTECH SERVICES

 Prudential and Market Conduct Regulations

 Fintech and Consumer Protection

Regulation

SUSTAINABLE DEVELOPMENT GOALS

The 2030 Sustainable Development Goals (SDGs) prominently position financial inclusion as an enabler of developmental goals.

8 of 17 SDGs feature financial inclusion as a target

SDG 1, 2, 3, 5, 8, 9,10, 17

INNOVATIONS TO SUPPORT FINTECH PRODUCTS AND SERVICES

- Mobile Phone/Internet Connectivity
- Cloud Computing
- Big Data Analytics
- Artificial Intelligence / Machine Learning

- Blockchain/Distributed Ledger Technology
- Application Programming Interface
- Quick Response (QR) Codes
- Internet of Things

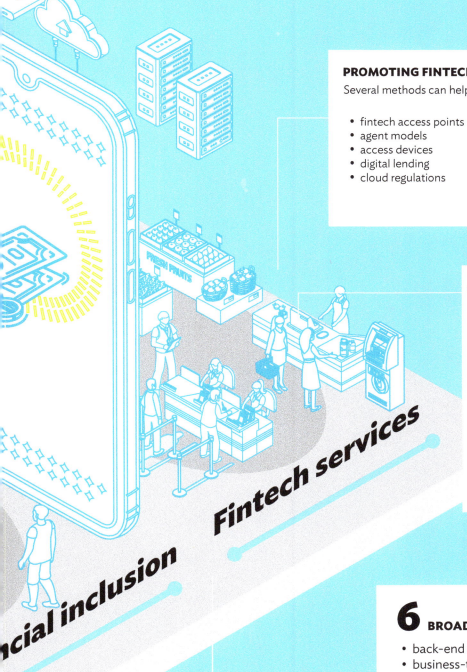

financial inclusion

Fintech services

PROMOTING FINTECH-ENABLED FINANCIAL SERVICES

Several methods can help enable fintech.

- fintech access points
- agent models
- access devices
- digital lending
- cloud regulations

- digital banking regulations
- open banking framework
- digital governmental payments
- digital merchant payments
- digital financial literacy

11 TYPES OF FINTECH SERVICES FOR FINANCIAL INCLUSION

- digital payments
- electronic money
- personal financial management and digital financial literacy tools
- digital savings products and services
- digital banking
- alternative digital finance and credit
- credit scoring and data analytics
- insurtech (insurance tech)
- digital and cryptocurrencies
- central bank digital currencies
- digital accounting and business tool providers

6 BROAD CATEGORIES OF FINTECH USERS

- back-end service providers for banks and insurance
- business-to-business
- business (including banks) to consumers
- government-to-business, business-to-government government-to-consumer, consumer-to-government
- business tools (including small and medium-sized enterprises)
- tools for consumers

INTRODUCTION

1

Digital financial services focused on innovative financial technologies (fintech) can benefit individuals, businesses, and governments. An appropriate policy and enabling regulatory environment for developing responsible and inclusive digital financial services can help expand inclusive economic growth and address the Sustainable Development Goals (SDGs).

Indeed, the rapid growth of fintech services in Asia and the Pacific has helped countries leapfrog the challenges of building traditional bricks-and-mortar financial services infrastructure and to dramatically increase access and use of these services. Fintech is also increasing the speed, security, and transparency of financial services.

An inclusive fintech ecosystem is recognized as an important tool to support economic growth, greater equality, and lower poverty levels. To achieve this, countries in this region can share their many experiences in developing appropriate policy and enabling regulatory approaches. These can support sound development of inclusive financial services while mitigating the risks of new fintech providers and technologies.

In light of the coronavirus disease (COVID-19) pandemic and its aftermath, digital access to financial services has become even more critical. As businesses and the general population have adapted to a digital lifestyle amid social distancing and quarantine measures, they are further embracing the convenience of remote access to financial services.

Digital payment platforms have helped many overcome the challenges of the pandemic. As the outbreak took hold, people shifted their activities to online transactions. And use of these platforms has surged around the region since then.

Many now hope that the new technologies can fuel economic recovery.

With appropriate legal and regulatory frameworks, policy makers and regulators hold the keys to enabling expansion of inclusive fintech services. To support this objective, this tool kit aims to help regulators and policy makers understand the following about fintech:

(i)   The latest developments: especially advances in payment technologies, blockchain, security and identity, personalized advice platforms, machine learning, artificial intelligence, cloud technologies, and open application programming interfaces (APIs).
(ii)   Support for financial inclusion, including access, use, and quality of services. This is especially so in digital payments, personal financial management, digital financial literacy tools, digital savings products and services, digital banking, alternative digital finance and credit, credit scoring and data analytics, insurance technologies, digital and crypto assets, and central bank digital currencies.
(iii) Support for the SDGs: this specifically includes those for ending hunger, achieving food security, and promoting sustainable agriculture, protecting health, gender equality and economic empowerment of women, economic growth and jobs, supporting industry, innovation, and infrastructure, reducing inequality, and building partnerships to implement the SDGs.
(iv)   Development of an appropriate regulatory and policy environment that looks at policy enablers, enabling technologies, and specific fintech activities.
(v)   Approaches to developing appropriate supervisory capacity, especially as it relates to regulatory technologies (regtech) and supervisory technologies (suptech).

Financial services have already begun to benefit from emerging and innovative digital technologies and will continue to do so. Tapping new fintech solutions, aided by strong policy and regulation, promises to create more inclusive growth and help economies recover from the COVID-19 pandemic.

FINTECH
LANDSCAPE
OVERVIEW

2

What Is Financial Technology?

Key messages

Financial technologies (fintech) are technology applications, processes, products, and services from both traditional and new financial service providers.

Fintech-enabled financial services focus on a wide range of categories that include payments, personal and financial management, credit, insurance, and savings, as well as enhancements to banking, regulations, and supervision.

Fintech firms use specialized software and algorithms on personal computers and, increasingly, smartphones. Companies, business owners, and consumers then use fintech to improve the management of financial operations and processes.

Initially, the term fintech was applied to back-end systems in traditional financial institutions. However, over the past decade, the focus has migrated toward front-end systems, consumer-oriented services and, increasingly, new financial players.

These services also impact a range of sectors and industries including:

- traditional banking services as well as personal financial management tools,
- investment services,
- insurance, and
- regulatory and supervisory technologies (or so-called regtech and suptech).

In addition, services encompass enabling agricultural value chains; access to health, education, and basic utilities; and even e-government and supporting "smart" cities. The list below and Figure 1 illustrate the rich array of services and trends.

Financial services using fintech:[1]

- payments (processing and networks);
- mobile wallets (e-money) and remittances;
- retail investing (robo-advisors);
- personal and wealth management;
- financial service automation;
- capital markets and institutional trading (including equity crowdfunding);
- core banking infrastructure ("cloud" providers);
- digital savings products and services;
- digital banking (neo banks, challenger banks, open banking, application programming interfaces [APIs]);
- security, fraud, and compliance-related providers (cybersecurity, anti-money laundering, and combating the financing of terrorism);
- alternative digital credit (marketplace, balance sheet, peer-to-peer [P2P], supply/trade finance);
- real estate and mortgage lending;
- credit scoring and data analytics;
- regulatory technologies and supervisory technologies (regtech/suptech);
- insurance technologies (insurtech);
- digital point-of-sale (POS) services;
- virtual and crypto assets;
- central bank digital currencies;
- blockchain and distributed ledger technologies; and
- digital accounting and business tools (including smart contracts).

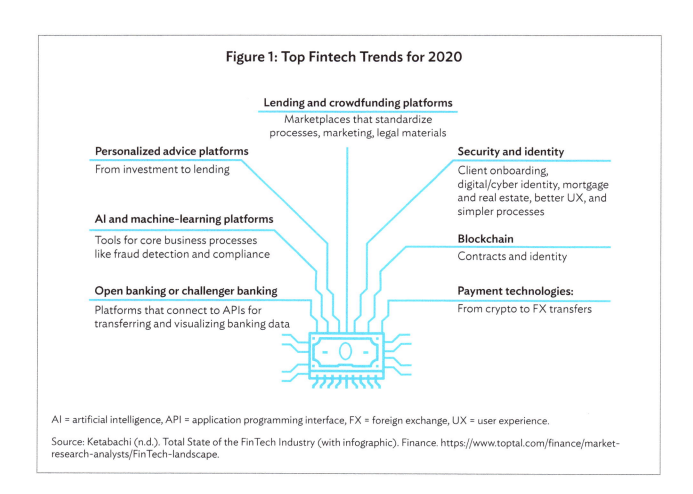

Figure 1: Top Fintech Trends for 2020

Lending and crowdfunding platforms
Marketplaces that standardize processes, marketing, legal materials

Personalized advice platforms
From investment to lending

Security and identity
Client onboarding, digital/cyber identity, mortgage and real estate, better UX, and simpler processes

AI and machine-learning platforms
Tools for core business processes like fraud detection and compliance

Blockchain
Contracts and identity

Open banking or challenger banking
Platforms that connect to APIs for transferring and visualizing banking data

Payment technologies:
From crypto to FX transfers

AI = artificial intelligence, API = application programming interface, FX = foreign exchange, UX = user experience.

Source: Ketabachi (n.d.). Total State of the FinTech Industry (with infographic). Finance. https://www.toptal.com/finance/market-research-analysts/FinTech-landscape.

---

[1] Note that initially most studies focused on various fintech verticals, but it is acknowledged that these services overlap and are increasingly horizontally linked.

Fintech Services and Financial Inclusion

Key messages

Fintech services focus on a wide range of categories. These include back-end service providers for banks and insurance, business-to-business, business (including banks)-to-consumers, government-to-business, business-to-government, government-to-consumer, consumer-to-government, business tools, and tools for consumers.

Fintech also has significant impact on financial inclusion by improving efficiency, lowering costs, and expanding access to financial services to more consumers than traditional brick-and-mortar financial service providers.

Historically, financial service institutions, especially banks, typically offered a full range of products and services, including payments, credit, savings, and related banking services. With fintech, financial products and services have generally been "unbundled" and are often now offered individually.[2] Innovation is often clustered into three categories:

- incremental (faster more efficient delivery of existing services);
- disruptive (Uber, Amazon); and
- transformative/breakthrough (internet).

Fintech's ability to streamline individual offerings with new technologies has improved efficiency, lowered costs, and expanded access to financial services to more consumers than traditional brick-and-mortar financial service providers. This is expanding financial inclusion more than was previously possible. A 2016 study by McKinsey Global Institute—estimates that digital financial services could expand access to formal financial accounts to 1.6 billion people in the world's developing economies. Such broader access could, in turn, help add 6% to gross domestic product in emerging economies by 2025 (Manyika et al. 2016).

---

[2] The one notable exception has been in the area of large technology providers, often referred as "Big Tech" firms (e.g., Alibaba, Tencent's WeChat, Grab, GoJek, Apple, Facebook, Google), which offer or plan to offer a range of services.

As such, fintech should be viewed more as "transformational" or "evolutionary," rather than "disruptive" of traditional financial service providers. In addition, rather than replacing or competing with the traditional banking sector, bank–fintech partnerships have emerged that can leverage new financial technologies within the banking sector.

Fintech users fall into six broad categories:

(i)   back-end service providers for banks and insurance;
(ii) business-to-business;
(iii) business (including banks)-to-consumers;
(iv) government-to-business, business-to-government, government-to-consumer, consumer-to-government;

(v)   business tools (including small and medium-sized enterprises); and
(vi) tools for consumers.

Advances in mobile banking; greater information, data, and more accurate analytics; and broader access will expand opportunities in each of these six categories.

Discussion of fintech services focused on financial inclusion include issues listed in Figure 3. More detailed descriptions can be found in Annex 1.

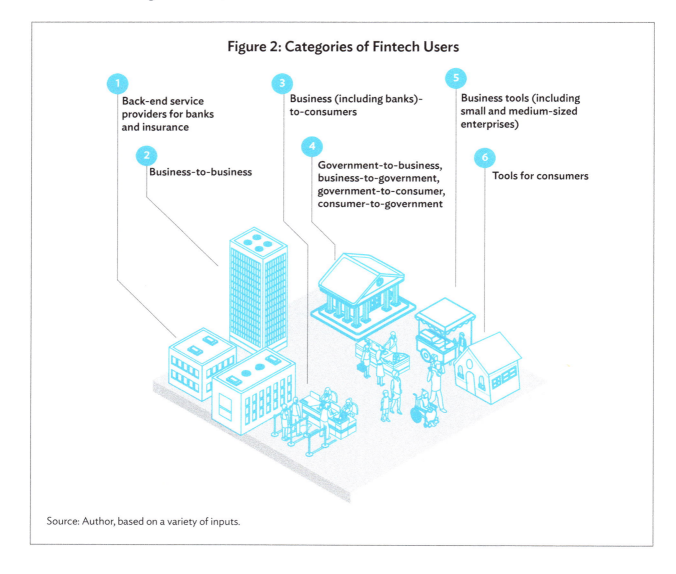

Figure 2: Categories of Fintech Users

1. Back-end service providers for banks and insurance
2. Business-to-business
3. Business (including banks)-to-consumers
4. Government-to-business, business-to-government, government-to-consumer, consumer-to-government
5. Business tools (including small and medium-sized enterprises)
6. Tools for consumers

Source: Author, based on a variety of inputs.

Figure 3: Fintech Services for Financial Inclusion

- Digital payments
- Electronic money
- Personal financial management and digital financial literacy tools
- Digital savings products and services
- Digital banking
- Alternative digital finance and credit

- Credit scoring and data analytics
- Insurance technology
- Digital and cryptocurrencies
- Central bank digital currencies
- Digital accounting and business tool providers

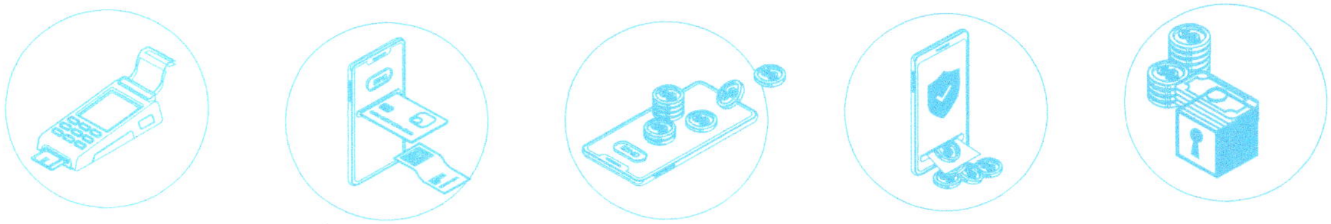

Source: Alliance for Financial Inclusion. Fintech for Financial Inclusion. https://www.afi-global.org/fintech-financial-inclusion.

New Technologies in Digital Finance

New technologies, such as machine learning/artificial intelligence (AI), predictive behavioral analytics, Internet of Things (IOT), and data-driven analysis and tools can improve access to financial products and services and personal financial management decision-making (Table 1).

"Learning" apps can reveal online behaviors that users themselves may be unaware of. With this information, these apps can provide customers with better financial tools to improve their automatic, unconscious spending and savings decisions, and provide SMEs better business management options.

Fintech also uses "chatbots" and AI to help customers with basic tasks and help businesses to reduce costs and improve inventory management and basic accounting services.

In addition, financial technologies are being used to combat fraud. Such fintech services leverage payment history information to flag unusual transactions. These tools not only improve regulatory compliance, fraud, and anti-money laundering, but can also help regulators.

Meanwhile, advances in regulatory technologies (regtech) and tools to help financial supervisors perform their jobs through new supervisory technologies (suptech) are improving regulatory oversight.

Advances in national retail payment systems that increasingly focus on interoperable and interconnected infrastructure support a move toward a more "cash-lite" society. Advances in e-money have allowed the creation of a range of new, simple transactional accounts that support stored-value and better payment and money transfer capabilities.

New back-end systems, especially "cloud" technologies, are also facilitating banking services. New digital banks and open banking via APIs are increasingly becoming tools to improve banking, and help leverage and interconnect traditional and new providers.

Numerous digital credit and finance models have been developed, both from existing banks, either directly or through partnerships, as well as new nonbank digital credit and finance platforms. Digital credit providers across Asia and the Pacific are increasingly utilizing a range of alternative data sources, such as airtime and e-money usage, transactional payment information, social media postings, location, and analysis of mobile phone interactions such as text data and user contact data, to enhance credit scoring and utilize data to monitor clients and improve collections.

Quick response (QR) codes are rapidly becoming one of the best mobile payment channels for the large-scale adoption of digital payments, given their relatively low cost compared to alternatives. Many countries across Asia are actively promoting QR-based payments. Most are choosing to support QR code standards, especially universal standards set by EMVCo.[3]

Technological innovations have proliferated in recent years (Table 1). Annex 1 provides more detailed descriptions of these technologies and their impact.

Table 1: Technology Innovations to Support Fintech Products and Services

Technology Innovation	Description	Impact on Fintech Financial Products and Services
Mobile Phone/Internet Connectivity	Mobile phones, especially smartphones and internet connectivity, have become essential distribution channels for financial products and services, allowing individuals and small and medium-sized enterprises (SMEs) to perform financial transactions anywhere at any time.	Mobile phones and internet connectivity are essential to digital financial products and services. Internet connectivity via personal computers and smartphones is improving information and knowledge management for individuals and SMEs. And mobile phone and internet data are expanding digital footprints that can be used to better support targeted digital financial products and services.
Cloud Computing	This provides computing storage, servers, and services over the internet. Cloud computing removes the burden of processing, accessing, and storing data from company servers and data centers, and puts it on remote servers. This information can then be reached on the internet whenever it is needed, through a connected device.	Cloud computing can provide significant benefits to large and small enterprises such as: • **Cost savings**—firms can place software applications in the cloud and thus limit ownership of IT infrastructure assets. • **Faster development and implementation of applications**—cloud computing significantly reduces time-to-market in application development from months to weeks or days. • **Scalability and agility**—enables firms to quickly scale computing resources.
Big Data Analytics	Big data refers to the exponential amount of structured and unstructured data generated continuously through different devices. The analytics of big data helps identify patterns, relationships, and interactions.	Big data analytics provides a wide range of opportunities for SMEs. These include better understanding of business processes, clients' needs, and overall characteristics of their markets. It also makes it easier and cheaper for banks, fintech firms, and Big Tech companies to assess business creditworthiness.
Artificial Intelligence (AI)/ Machine Learning (ML)	AI is the analysis of data to model some aspect of the world with computers, and models that learn from the data to respond intelligently to new data and adapt outputs accordingly. ML is the set of techniques and tools that allow computers to "think" by creating mathematical algorithms based on accumulated data.	AI and ML can unlock value from the vast amount of data in the databases of traders, banks, logistics companies, and others that could— combined with alternative data sources—be algorithmically predictive in guiding risk management to unlock SME finance. Credit scoring models using AI and ML make it possible to serve SMEs that previously had no access to finance.

continued on next page

---

[3] See https://www.emvco.com/emv-technologies/qrcodes/

Table 1 continued

Technology Innovation	Description	Impact on Fintech Financial Products and Services
Blockchain/Distributed Ledger Technology (DLT)	As a form of DLT, blockchain presents a global decentralized database. It is secured through cryptography and runs on millions of devices that anyone can access. Importantly, using blockchain removes the need for expensive intermediaries in transactions between two parties, and thus substantially reduces or even eliminates transaction costs.	Blockchain can help financial services better target SMEs in many ways, from filling know-your-customer or KYC gaps to broadening the information for credit assessment and reducing loan risk, as well as trade finance. With a single mechanism for tracking steps in the trade finance process—orders, contracts, documentation, shipments, customs, delivery—it could enhance interoperability among previously incompatible systems, improving accuracy and eliminating redundancy.
Application Programming Interface (API)	By allowing one program to communicate with another, APIs create the potential for many innovative products and services used by millions of people daily.	Open APIs are the major enabling technology behind the Open Banking initiative that is transforming the financial services sector, and can ultimately help SMEs transform digitally, by allowing fintech firms to provide customized products and services to businesses.
Quick Response (QR) Codes	QR codes are a type of two-dimensional barcode that offers faster reading time and more information storage.	With QR codes, SMEs do not need to purchase expensive point-of-sale or electronic data capture terminals to accept payments, thus lowering operating costs. QR codes also offer a user experience at least as good as cash, if not better. Individual users and SMEs which use QR codes in their business do not need financial education to use QR codes for payments.
Internet of Things (IOT)	IOT refers to the billions of physical devices around the world that are now and can potentially be connected to the internet to collect, generate, and share data.	IOT offers many benefits for SMEs and large firms. These include operational efficiency, better understanding of customers to deliver enhanced and customized services, better decision-making, and increased business value.

Source: G20 Global Policy for Financial Inclusion (2020). *Promoting Digital and Innovative SME Financing*. Washington, DC: International Bank for Reconstruction and Development/World Bank. https://www.gpfi.org/sites/gpfi/files/saudi_digitalSME.pdf

In addition, other new technologies support the expansion of insurance, such as weather indexes for crop insurance (Box 1).

Box 1: Harnessing Weather Index Crop Insurance for Small Farmers

The Asian Development Bank (ADB) completed a weather index-based crop insurance pilot in 2019 in three districts in Bangladesh involving over 9,500 smallholder rice farmers.

Crop insurance is particularly valuable given the unpredictable effects of climate change on farming. It can be considered a climate adaptation tool, allowing farmers to plan and put aside money for emergency use when harvests are suddenly damaged or destroyed. In addition, using crop insurance, farmers can raise their productivity and income through investments in innovative technologies.

The ADB grant featured innovative components that included:

Mobile banking for claims settlements

Management Information System to digitalize the whole crop insurance process

Weather stations

(i)   mobile banking services for collecting insurance premiums and payment of claims;
(ii)   development of parametric weather indices for claims settlement without on-the-spot assessment of crop damage following excess or deficit rainfall; and
(iii) installation of automated weather stations for providing climate-related information.

Source: ADB (2019). The Future of Inclusive Finance. Welcome address by Bambang Susantono. ADB Vice-President for Knowledge Management. 6 November. https://www.adb.org/sites/default/files/publication/643831/3rd-asia-finance-forum-conference-proceedings.pdf.

Regulation and Promoting Fintech Financial Services

Key messages

Proportionate and risk-based policies and regulations are key to providing an appropriate enabling environment to support the development of responsible fintech services.

Approaches include fintech-enabling regulations and policies, regulating enabling technologies, or regulating specific fintech products and services.

Regulators and policy makers can more actively support fintech through public–private partnerships and dialogues, support for innovation hubs, and regulatory sandboxes.

Several methods that can enable fintech are available

Regulation

As technology is integrated into financial services and new financial service providers are created, legal and regulatory frameworks have evolved to regulate and provide appropriate oversight for the growing sector.

An appropriate regulatory-enabling environment can facilitate responsible development of fintech. This includes appropriate, proportionate, and risk-based approaches to regulations and policies and to robust oversight and supervision policies and measures. Some of the most important policies that affect fintech include:

- proportionate anti-money laundering/combating the financing of terrorism (Financial Action Task Force on Money Laundering Compliance),[4]
- tiered know-your-customer (KYC) regulations,
- e-money operator regulations and guidelines,
- remote account opening rules,
- agent regulations (for banks and nonbank financial institutions),
- fair access to information communication technologies,
- retail payment systems laws and regulations (including new developments with

---

[4]   Risk-based and proportionate regulation. Regulators should adopt a philosophy of risk-based and proportionate regulation, with the regulatory burden reflective of the probability and potential magnitude of harm to clients based on the consumer protection risks identified. For more information see, the Centre for Financial Inclusion's Handbook on Consumer Protection for Inclusive Finance at https://www.smartcampaign.org/storage/documents/handbook_Consumer_Protection_Inclusive_Finance_FINAL.pdf; also see https://medium.com/kyc-io-scalable-kyc-management-solutions/what-is-risk-based-approach-rba-in-kyc-aml-9e5173846fb9.

standardized QR codes and the importance of interoperable and open systems),
- digital and open finance regulations,
- rules on blockchain and distributed ledger technologies,
- technology-embedded supervision,
- licensing of nonbank digital credit providers,
- competition policies,
- security and fraud mitigation, and
- consumer protection regulations.

Table 2 outlines the approach to fintech used at the Bank for International Settlements (BIS).

New risks include the challenges of growing interconnection in financial systems and the increasing number of financial providers (some completely new to the financial system) as well as technology failure, human error, and fraud. According to research by the Bill & Melinda Gates Foundation, human error accounts for about 70% of risk for consumers and malfeasance accounts for about 80% of risk for fintech providers. Liquidity/solvency risk—predominantly whether consumers

can access their funds when they need them, rather than the safety of those deposits—is the major issue e-money and new payment providers face, as well as some agent banking models.

Business models for success in fintech services differ significantly from more traditional brick-and-mortar financial service providers. For these services, it is crucial for policy makers and regulators to ensure a level and enabling playing field. To do so, however, they require understanding of the business models and incentives that private sector fintech providers are using. With this knowledge, the authorities can develop "smart" policies and regulations that encourage innovation, while at the same time provide safety and soundness in the financial system. With deeper understanding of the relative risks of low-value, high-volume fintech transactions, for instance, regulators can design better, simplified, and tiered electronic KYC and customer due diligence requirements. These can lower the barriers to entry that typically hinder customers and providers.

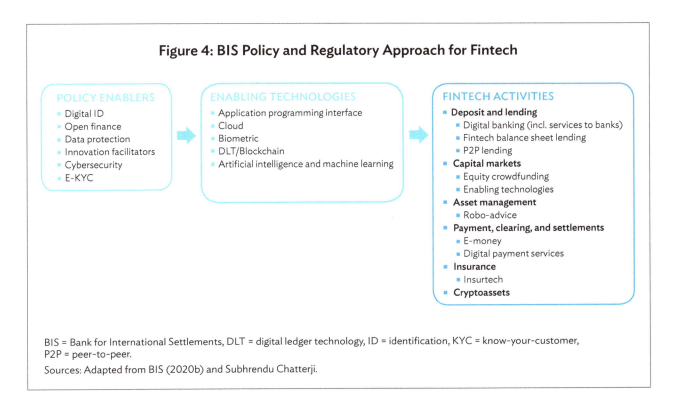

Figure 4: BIS Policy and Regulatory Approach for Fintech

POLICY ENABLERS
- Digital ID
- Open finance
- Data protection
- Innovation facilitators
- Cybersecurity
- E-KYC

ENABLING TECHNOLOGIES
- Application programming interface
- Cloud
- Biometric
- DLT/Blockchain
- Artificial intelligence and machine learning

FINTECH ACTIVITIES
- **Deposit and lending**
  - Digital banking (incl. services to banks)
  - Fintech balance sheet lending
  - P2P lending
- **Capital markets**
  - Equity crowdfunding
  - Enabling technologies
- **Asset management**
  - Robo-advice
- **Payment, clearing, and settlements**
  - E-money
  - Digital payment services
- **Insurance**
  - Insurtech
- **Cryptoassets**

BIS = Bank for International Settlements, DLT = digital ledger technology, ID = identification, KYC = know-your-customer, P2P = peer-to-peer.
Sources: Adapted from BIS (2020b) and Subhrendu Chatterji.

It is also important that authorities foster an environment that encourages fintech and traditional financial service providers to cooperate and even form partnerships. This will allow them to deliver a deeper range of financial products and services, not just credit, savings, and payments, but also remittances and insurance. Tensions may exist, especially between banks and nonbank financial institutions, but cooperation and service level agreements among players will be necessary to leverage infrastructure and core competencies, and broaden the range of financial services. Fintech regulation must keep pace as services evolve, especially in new partnerships.

In addition, regulators are reinventing how they engage with the fintech sector and are innovating, including through innovation offices, test-and-learn approaches, and regulatory sandboxes.

Typically, it is innovation offices, which can facilitate engagement between regulators and innovators, that get regulatory innovation underway, according to the United Nations Secretary-General's Special Advocate for Inclusive Finance for Development. Through the dialogue that these offices generate, greater understanding is gained of the technology-enabled financial innovations in question, and of the regulatory responses that will be most appropriate. The offices can reduce the uncertainty that may hinder the regulatory progress and indicate to innovators that regulators have adopted a pro-innovation stance. This can help encourage inclusive fintech.

Among the important lessons of innovation offices, therefore, is that early and regular engagement with innovators is important. When there is "executive buy-in" for interagency coordination, this can improve functioning and provide powerful support to regulators as they pursue financial inclusion. Meanwhile, through eligibility criteria, regulators can prioritize engagement with financial service providers in the market that they deem crucial for reaching their goals. Nonetheless, the quality of innovation offices rests on the quality of resources, including the technical capabilities of their own staff (UN

Secretary-General's Special Advocate for Inclusive Finance for Development and CCAF 2019).

Regulatory sandboxes, previously known as test-and-learn approaches, can create "safe spaces" for fintech providers to test new products and services, business models, and delivery mechanisms, without needing to comply with all the usual regulatory requirements.

Governments can also drive financial inclusion and fintech ecosystems by disbursing salaries and social payments as well as accepting payments electronically. Interoperability is considered important to support a fintech ecosystem; however, the consensus is that interoperability should be market-driven. Through regular dialogue with all private sector players, regulators can identify the best timing for interoperability and stay on top of players' concerns. Typically, these concerns focus on recovering investment costs of being an early fintech provider, boosting volumes, or remaining competitive. They are also concerned with retaining customers and increasing value-added services. Nonetheless, regulators are aware that they may need to take a more active role where interoperability is absent, and thus impedes progress. Market development and the readiness of players to compete while remaining profitable will determine which solutions to apply.

Among the possible solutions is price sharing, in which the initial investor gets a bigger portion of fees or profits and "sunset" provisions, in which exclusivity is time-bound. Establishing a framework for competitors to interact, meanwhile, can also increase competition. Setting standards can also facilitate interoperability, especially as regulators develop better national retail payment systems and harness new technologies such as QR codes (Box 2).

Regulating virtual and crypto assets is also a challenge for regulators. In initial coin offerings, start-ups have gained a new way to raise funds from investors that presents fresh challenges.

Such offerings went unregulated in many countries, and thus invited scams and fraud. This lack of oversight also allowed entrepreneurs to bypass security and exchange commissions by

Box 2: A National QR Code Standard for Payments in the Philippines

In line with its thrust of ensuring the efficiency of payment systems in support of inclusive economic development, the Monetary Board of the Bangko Sentral ng Pilipinas (BSP) is requiring the adoption of a National Quick Response (QR) Code Standard for payments. The standard, according to BSP, is necessary to ensure interoperability of QR-enabled payment and financial services.

QR technology has emerged as the most convenient and cost-efficient means of moving funds from one account to another. Interoperable QR codes have been gaining traction as an alternative to traditional debit and credit cards. A QR code contains most if not all critical information such as account name and account number required in a payment instruction. The code thus minimizes encoding errors. Moreover, it is faster and easier to just scan the code than to dip or swipe a card and sign a charge slip.

A national QR code standard, it is hoped, will encourage more small enterprises to join the financial system. Merchants can simply scan and print the new codes and display them for scanning by clients. This offers a much more affordable way to invest in electronic data capture equipment, such as the point-of-sale terminals typically required for card-based payments.

Source: BSP (2019).

disguising their offerings as "utility tokens," thus avoiding relevant fees and costs. Bad accounting practices, misleading information, and outright fraud also weighed on many initial coin offerings. In response, including to increasing concerns about crypto assets, most jurisdictions have tightened regulations around them or banned them altogether (Nasdaq 2020).

The Financial Action Task Force (FATF) recently updated its guidance to regulators and policy makers on all virtual assets and virtual asset service providers (VASPs) which include crypto assets and crypto asset exchanges broadening the supervision of crypto assets. The new FATF guidelines are comprehensive and include the requirement that countries that allow VASPs to operate must properly license or register them and subject them to appropriate supervision and monitoring. The guidance also requires that all VASPs be subject to the same FATF standards that apply to all financial institutions.[5]

In addition, blockchain technologies and the use of distributed ledgers open up new ways to supervise financial risks. This includes a new approach for "technology embedded supervision." This allows authorities to automatically monitor developments by reading the market's ledger. Firms then face less need to collect verify, and deliver data (Box 3).

No single or comprehensive approach can address the problems of the emerging fintech industry. Its diverse offerings require diverse solutions. So far, however, most governments have used existing regulations, and sometimes adapted them to the specific regulatory needs of fintech. Nonetheless, the General Data Protection Regulation (GDPR) in the European Union (EU) is one new approach. The GDPR is designed to govern the collection and use of personal data to protect customers using many of the emerging fintech products. Several, countries where initial coin offerings are popular, such as Japan, have taken the lead in developing regulations for such offerings to protect investors.

While regulations to address P2P lending models have developed in the United States (US), the United Kingdom (UK), and the EU—and now in Indonesia, the PRC, and the Philippines—regulators have also been working closely with the industry to develop codes of conduct. Notable examples include the codes of conduct of the Marketplace Lenders Association[6] and the Small Business Borrowers' Bill of Rights.[7]

---

[5] See Updated Guidance for Risk-Based Approach for Virtual Assets and Virtual Asset Service Providers, FATF 28 Oct 2021. https://www.fatf-gafi.org/publications/fatfrecommendations/documents/guidance-rba-virtual-assets-2021.html
[6] Marketplace Lending Association. http://marketplacelendingassociation.org.
[7] Responsible Business Lending Coalition. http://www.responsiblebusinesslending.org.

Box 3: Regulating Blockchain Finance BIS on Technology-Embedded Supervision

The spread of distributed ledger technology into financial services has the potential to improve supervisory efficiency and quality, according to the Bank for International Settlements (BIS). "Technology embedded supervision," as a regulatory framework, could encourage "tokenized" markets to comply with automatic monitoring of transactions through the reading of a market's ledger. Such supervision would reduce the need for firms themselves to collect, verify, and deliver data. The paper explores the conditions under which distributed ledger data might be used to monitor compliance. It models a decentralized market to replace current intermediary-based verification of legal data with blockchain-enabled data credibility based on economic consensus. The paper also looks at the conditions for gaining market economic consensus strong enough to guarantee transactions are economically final and that could gain supervisors' trust in the distributed ledgers' data.

BIS = Bank for International Settlements.
Source: BIS (2019a).

In markets such as in Indonesia, the PRC, and the Philippines, abusive collection practices, such as harassing customers on social media, have emerged, raising concerns about consumer protection (Business and Human Rights Resource Centre 2019). Due to risks faced by small investors,[8] some countries have restricted P2P platforms from raising capital from small individual investors to avoid risks (Financial Services Authority 2017).

Areas where regulation can support fintech ecosystems

Several methods can help enable fintech. These include (i) fintech access points, (ii) agent models, (iii) access devices, (iv) digital lending, (v) cloud regulations, (vi) digital banking regulations, (vii) open banking/finance frameworks, (viii) digital governmental payments, (ix) digital merchant payments, and (x) digital financial literacy. Each of these is discussed.

Some countries are also experimenting with "centers of excellence" (Box 4).

Fintech access points

One precondition for increasing fintech use is to ensure broadly available fintech-enabled access points. According to the Findex surveys, "distance to financial service providers" was the second most important demand-side issue adults cited to explain why they do not have an account in a financial institution (the most important demand-side issues were the high costs and challenges associated with opening and holding an account) (World Bank 2019b).

Countries with advanced banking and payment systems have usually measured access via the number of ATMs, point-of-sale (POS) machines, and credit/debit cards issued. However, with advances in fintech access points increasingly including mobile phone-based access (especially with the advent of smartphones), the ability to leapfrog traditional payment access points has changed dramatically, and previous metrics to measure access points have changed significantly.

---

[8] For more information, see Ezubao on https://en.wikipedia.org/wiki/Ezubao.

Box 4: OJK Infinity (Indonesia)

In "centers of excellence" in several parts of Indonesia, fintech firms, regulators, experts, and academics are coming together to discuss industry trends, conduct research, and gain skills. The country's Financial Services Authority (OJK) established the Innovation Centre for Digital Technology—OJK Infinity—in August 2018 as a fintech research center for business owners, enterprises, government officials, and academics to collaborate. It aims for a "more friendly fintech ecosystem in Indonesia and to encourage any business maker to build the digital financial system that will facilitate the society."

OJK Infinity focuses on:

- education centers,
- digital financial industry ecosystem development,
- fintech incubation, and
- sources of information

Source: IndonesiaGO Digital (2019).

Agent models

Agent models can be separated into bank agent models and nonbank agent models, with the latter focused on e-money cash-in/cash-out services. In the agent banking model, banks provide financial services through grocery stores, retail outlets, post offices, and other nonbank agents (Box 5). Banks can thus expand services into areas with insufficient incentives to get involved or in which they lack capacity for a formal branch. This stands to benefit the many people who are "unbanked" in rural and poor areas.

Many countries see agent banking for its potential to provide poor and rural areas with access to formal financial services, with varying success in recent years. Brazil, a recognized pioneer in the area, has put in place a mature network of agent banks in most municipalities, setting an example for the rest of Latin America. Likewise, banks in Africa and Asia and the Pacific are following suit.

Nonbank agent models have been offered extensively by nonbank electronic money issuers, especially those offering mobile e-money services in parts of Asia. The design and implementation of agent models—as well as the regulation, supervision, and oversight of agent operations—vary widely across countries and regions. This is clear in the variety of services offered, in the types of businesses acting as agents, and in the financial institutions working through agents. It is evident in the business structures employed to manage them, and whether agents are limited to e-money cash-in/cash-out services or a more extensive level of basic banking services. These differences contribute to the varied success of agent models in bridging the financial inclusion gap.

Access devices

Access device innovations are also making payments and financial transactions more convenient. The most commonly used access device, the payment card, however, is changing rapidly: from plastic cards with embossed names and numbers, to magnetic stripe cards with data, to smart cards with integrated circuit chips, to cards with contactless connectivity and/or multiple purposes (ID, generation of authorization credentials, virtual cards now on mobile devices).

Box 5: Impact of Agent Banking on Financial Inclusion in Malaysia

Bank Negara Malaysia launched a framework for agent banking in August 2012 to reach rural populations with no access to bank branches.

Agent banking services are restricted only to unserved and underserved areas for Malaysian citizens. Underserved areas are identified based on subdistricts (*mukims*) with more than 2,000 people, or in the case of Sabah, *Dewan Undangan Negeri*, which have no more than five access points.

During the initial phase of agent banking, only a limited number of financial services were allowed. The scale was expanded in 2015 as a response to the greater demand from customers and agents. In 2011, only 46% of the subdistricts in Malaysia had access to financial services, but 97% had access 3 years later after agent banking had been implemented.

As such, this is an excellent example of using technology and working with the private sector to achieve a public good, ensuring that the desired objectives are achieved through well-designed regulations.

Source: Bhunia (2017).

Mobile phones and mobile devices, however, are playing a bigger role in many emerging markets than traditional payment cards as an access device. Low-cost smartphones are driving even more ways to support digital financial services, and to support mobile POS and QR code payments that offer an alternative to traditional POS devices. Payment kiosks and other self-service devices are helping to bridge technology between brick-and-mortar branches and entirely digital payment platforms.

Regulators need to understand the different devices fintech providers are using and the security risks these platforms create. The International Organization for Standardization (ISO) has issued several guidelines on standards, especially for mobile financial services.[9]

Digital lending

As noted, the data created by early-adopting individuals and SMEs as they use payment platforms, social networks, and mobile applications could aid credit decisions by bank and nonbank fintech credit providers. Credit reporting agencies have begun using alternative data to evaluate creditworthiness. Use of such services can help increase the chances for individuals and SMEs to gain access to financing (International Finance Corporation [IFC] 2017).

Traditional lending is being transformed as providers of digital credit automate tasks including underwriting, loan servicing, or compliance with regulation. This lowers prices for financial services and reduces the time needed to serve individual users and small businesses. Additionally, information asymmetry is falling and new sources of information for assessing credit risk are emerging as firms increasingly turn to alternative data and advanced data analytics and artificial intelligence.

However, promoting the use of alternative data and alternative nonbank lending comes with challenges that need to be considered when defining policies for encouraging the use of alternative data for increasing digital credit (IFC 2017). These include:

---

[9] See the ISO online browsing platform at https://www.iso.org/obp/ui/#iso:std:iso:12812:-1:ed-1:v1:en.

Improving the availability and accuracy of alternative data. Considering the different sources of data used for credit scoring analysis, there is a need to ensure the accuracy of information to share this with credit information-sharing agencies. As noted, access to a digital ID system for individual users and SMEs is key (see earlier section on digital ID infrastructure).

Authorities could also encourage automation of data collection to broaden availability and raise quality, ensuring data are updated and accessible. This is especially true of government data sources, such as filing of taxes, company registrations, and other government payment histories. This could widen the digital data footprint for individuals and SMEs.

Expanding coverage of credit reporting service providers as well as enabling responsible cross-border data exchanges. To benefit from the vast amount of data generated, and that could increase the access to finance for individual users and SMEs, credit information sharing by credit reporting service providers needs to expand to allow use of alternative data and to broaden the range of credit providers who can access credit reporting services.

Regulators in several markets are both broadening the range of financial service providers which report and share credit data as well as promoting the expanded use of alternative data by credit reporting service providers. This includes promoting information sharing between these providers and/or the use of open data platforms with other data repositories (like court records, company registries, collateral registries).

Developing standards to encourage the responsible sharing of digital data across borders is also important over the medium term. Barriers to data sharing could arise from different regulations and formats, and standard digital IDs for individual users and SMEs will also have to be addressed to enable the use of cross-border digital information sharing. Regional coordination among regulators and policy makers to improve comparability and ensure consistency of digital data shared across countries will be essential.

The BIS Task Force on Data Sharing, and other organizations that set standards, can help to advance such collaboration and encourage coordination (BIS 2015b).

Establishing principles for responsible use of AI. Fintech firms have tapped AI—combined with traditional and alternative data—to develop highly sophisticated credit assessment models that can evaluate customer ability and willingness to pay. Some of these alternative models have so far proved highly accurate. Concerns have risen, however, about potential biases and inexplicability of results in some of these models.

Policy makers and regulators could consider the establishment of principles that guide responsible use of AI. Regulators in different places have started to publish general approaches to the use of AI and specific guidelines directed to the financial sector.

As it relates to the risk of potential bias in the data used in credit risk models, an important reason for the bias is that AI–machine learning algorithms may be trained with data sets that do not include all income levels or types of firms (in the case of SME borrowers). To address this issue, the EU, for example, published guidelines on ethics in AI in April 2019, which will lead to further legislative proposals (European Parliament 2019).

The Monetary Authority of Singapore has also introduced the Principles to Promote Fairness, Ethics, Accountability and Transparency in the Use of AI and Data Analytics in Singapore's Financial Sector (Monetary Authority of Singapore, n.d.).

As noted above, nonbank alternative fintech lenders have gained momentum over the past decade, with especially high growth rates in some countries, providing a new source of funding for unbanked and underbanked individuals and SMEs. This rapid development of nonbank digital lending platforms has already given rise to problems associated with platform failures and fraudulent activities. Nevertheless, according to a recent survey conducted by the World Bank and the Cambridge Centre for Alternative Finance (CCAF), only 22% of jurisdictions formally regulate nonbank alternative lenders (World Bank and CCAF 2019).

In some cases, nonbank alternative lending providers and platforms have been included in existing regulations, are prohibited, or are operating without regulatory oversight. When approaching regulatory reforms or drafting new regulation, at least the following areas should be considered: registration, licensing and reporting, investor protection and securities laws, clearing settlement and segregation of client money, capital requirements, data protection, credit analysis, and underwriting.

Cloud regulations

The regulatory environment for use of cloud computing technology to support financial services has changed dramatically over the past few years. Cloud technology has evolved rapidly along with improvements in the maturity of cloud security features and controls. Financial regulators across the Association of Southeast Asian Nations (ASEAN), have approved and expanded rules around cloud computing.

From a regulatory perspective, four critical aspects of cloud operations require understanding and attention, as regulators adapt policies to allow cloud computing. These include the following:

- **Outsourcing.** Strong contractual obligations need to address data regulations, right to audit, exit strategy, concentration risk, service provider key performance indicators, and conduct material outsourcing assessments.
- **Operational risk mitigation.** Need to address systemic risk across areas such as business continuity, disaster recovery, security, data, infrastructure, service delivery, and ability to demonstrate that financial institutions are aware of their risk exposure, and are on the way to mitigate these risks and reduce exposures.
- **Internal governance.** Prior to implementation of the solution, organizations are required to ensure that internal governance forums, risk committees, local operational committees, and local executive committees within the organization approve

the solution and assessments prior to obtaining regulatory approval.
- **Risk operating model.** There must be an ongoing risk function to ensure ongoing compliance with the regulations and contractually (Finextra 2019).

Digital banking regulations

Since 2014, digital banking penetration has increased from 150% to 300% across emerging markets in Asia and the Pacific. The percentage of digitally active customers doubled during this period, and some 52% of urban bank customers in emerging Asian countries currently use digital banking services. Across Asia, more than 700 million consumers use digital banking regularly (Mondato 2019). The current coronavirus disease (COVID-19) pandemic has also spurred growth and interest in digital banking.

Many regulators and policy makers across Asia are developing regulations to support new forms of digital or virtual banks. These are seen as offering convenience, ease, and speed, especially for the new breed of digital consumers who prefer to bank via their mobile phones. Digital bank customers are able to bank anywhere at any time, needing no physical branches (Box 6). In addition, since digital banks have lower overhead costs, they can offer higher interest rates on savings accounts and lower fees, and even faster loan processing.

Open banking/finance frameworks

By using open banking and APIs, third parties can connect with banks and access customer data through standardized protocols, allowing fintech companies to provide new products and services and to create new business models. In doing so, they are also contributing to the collaborative effort of innovation, to creating new ecosystems, and to smarter data use.

Since nonbank financial institutions play key roles, there is also now a trend and need beyond open banking to support open finance frameworks. This new trend broadens the range of financial players that can share data

Box 6: Internet-Only Banks to Change the Financial Landscape in the Republic of Korea

A shift from traditional finance to digital finance can help promote financial inclusion by lowering the costs for financial services even in a highly regulated financial environment. Such is the case in the Republic of Korea where two internet-only banks have emerged to challenge the traditional banking sector.

Other countries keen to boost competition in the financial sector, or expand financial services to underserved areas and people unable to travel to physical buildings, could learn lessons from the Korean experience with this type of banking.

Source: Kim (2016).

and includes companies such as insurance companies, pensions, as well as large payment providers or e-money issuers, e-commerce providers, and even utility companies.

It may be too soon to draw conclusions, however, as many open banking and now open finance regulations only became effective since 2018. While there is no single model or solution to open banking and open finance frameworks, several standards are now developing that can assist policy makers and regulators in developing a roadmap. These new standards can help create a facilitative ecosystem of secure exchange of data between banks and other financial service providers and third parties.

While models may differ on the approach and scope, common standards and principles are now being developed and utilized in several markets. Regulators are increasingly co-opting industry working groups to ensure responsible governing bodies, often jointly overseen by financial regulators, are in place. These early regulatory efforts have concentrated on defining standardized API frameworks, creating governance bodies and rules, enhancing security, developing infrastructure, establishing authentication methods, ensuring liability arrangements and developing data privacy and consumer protection standards.

Analyzing current frameworks and adapting to the local context and maturity of a country might be a first approach toward defining an open banking or finance framework. Note that even where the approach to open banking or finance is regulator-driven, enhanced collaboration with financial

institutions and fintechs is relevant to ensure general acceptance and adoption of standards. Also, moving toward international open finance standards is expected to result in better regional and ultimately international interoperability.

Finally, regulators might consider opening up customers´ data access to other sectors beyond the financial sector, moving from open banking toward open economies, that increase data-driven ecosystems and create a level playing field.

Digital governmental payments

Governments play a key role in supporting inclusive fintech ecosystems. Not only do they play a role as a key coordinator, but more importantly government use of digital payments is crucial for building trust and driving transaction volumes. These include not only making payments across the governmental agencies, but also to individuals and businesses as well as receiving payments (Better Than Cash Alliance 2017).

Digital merchant payments

A viable pricing model and acceptance fees low enough to incentivize use are needed to achieve scale and thus encourage merchants and other SMEs to use digital payments. This is particularly important for smaller SMEs and informal retailers wishing to accept digital payments, whether face-to-face or online. To foster this, regulators could consider encouraging fintech, especially payment service providers, to cap or limit merchant transaction fees.

Among the incentives for higher acceptance levels is disallowing surcharges on transactions that could eventually be passed on to the merchant, or even subsidizing the cost of acceptance in the early stages of development. Additionally, enhancing market transparency through disclosure of exchange fees, rates, and other commissions would result in more efficient markets and encourage adoption of digital payments.

Some countries have also had success in using upper-limit thresholds on single-payment cash transactions by consumers. However, challenges remain even for the e-commerce sector, where a large percentage of transactions are still cash on delivery. Advances and the experiences of digital payments in the PRC demonstrate potential for other countries in Asia.

Digital financial literacy

Financial literacy tools, especially those that promote awareness and use of digital financial services, can enhance adoption. Effective tools should provide simple instructions on how digital financial services work, with a clear understanding of the benefits and risks. Some countries are using chatbots.

Related to financial literacy, as noted, is the need for an enhanced consumer protection framework that covers the unique aspects of digital financial services, and establishes regulations that protect consumer funds that are clear and uniform. Also needed are redress mechanisms and access to information to better support trust and adoption of digital financial services and help promote a fintech ecosystem.

Finally, consumer fees should not deter use, but should be affordable, even for the financially underserved. Measures such as discounts, cash rebates, rewards, or loyalty programs could be considered to support this, especially for government-sponsored initiatives.

Fintech and the Sustainable Development Goals

Financial inclusion is central to the 2030 Sustainable Development Goals (SDGs), and is included in the targets of 8 of the 17 SDGs. SDG 1 calls for eradicating poverty and SDG 2 aims to end hunger, achieve food security, and promote sustainable agriculture. Financial inclusion is also factor in the following SDG goals: SDG 3 on protecting health; SDG 5 on gender equality and economic empowerment of women; SDG 8 on economic growth and jobs; SDG 9 on supporting industry, innovation, and infrastructure; and SDG 10 on reducing inequality. In SDG 17, on strengthening the means of implementation, there is hope that greater financial inclusion can fuel economic growth.

Academic evidence suggests that broadening financial inclusion can help fuel economic growth even as it contributes to efforts to reach the SDGs (ADB 2018). A recent report from McKinsey Global Institute, for example, points to digital finance benefiting billions of people in the likely impact it would have on inclusive growth, which would contribute $3.7 trillion to gross domestic product among developing economies in a period of 10 years (McKinsey Global Institute 2016).

The potential impact of mobile financial services on poverty is also strong. Kenyan mobile money provider, M-Pesa, by increasing access and use of mobile e-money services, has helped lead many households out of poverty. It has made economic life better for poor women and members of female-headed households, a recent study suggests.[10,11]

Financial inclusion is also helping to stabilize financial systems and economies, mobilizing domestic resources through national savings and raising government revenues via better tax collection.

---

[10] In Kenya, a long-term impact study looking at M-Pesa found that mobile money use lifted some 194,000 households (2% of the population) out of poverty.

[11] In particular, the United Nations Capital Development Fund (UNCDF) notes growing evidence that access to digitally enabled savings leads to positive economic outcomes for women, including increasing productivity and profits and greater investment in their businesses. Having savings also makes women less likely to sell assets to address health emergencies, stabilizes their incomes during economic shocks, and provides them greater control over their funds (UNCDF n.d.).

Figure 5: 8 of 17 SDG Goals Feature Financial Inclusion as Key Enabler

Source: See the Financial Inclusion and the SDGs, United National Development Fund. https://www.uncdf.org/financial-inclusion-and-the-sdgs.

FOUNDATIONAL INFRASTRUCTURE AND POLICY ENVIRONMENT

3

Foundational Infrastructure

Identification infrastructure

Access to financial services is severely hampered
in many countries by the lack of adequate
identification (ID) infrastructure. Adequate
access by financial service providers to ID
infrastructure is important in supporting financial
inclusion and minimizing risks of fraud, and
encouraging compliance with Anti-Money
Laundering and Counter-Terrorism Financing
(AML-CTF) regulations. Digital and biometric
identification technologies can also help financial
service providers make better decisions. Some
promising developments in several key markets
include integrating payment infrastructure with
ID infrastructure to support efficiency gains, and
the creation of digital payment histories for credit
scoring. The Aadhaar ID system in India and
digital ID issued by Pakistan's National Database
and Registration Authority are good examples.
Both systems have pros and cons, which policy
makers must consider (Highet 2016).

Notably, the World Bank and other institutions
have been working on digital ID standards that
governments and policy makers should consider
as they develop national digital ID systems
(World Bank 2017a). The World Bank provides
guidance to advance the promotion of robust
and inclusive digital identification systems,
and these principles encourage the facilitation
of customer identification for digital financial
services (World Bank 2017b). In developing
national digital ID systems, governments should
help ensure universal coverage and accessibility;

remove barriers to access and usage; and ensure that identification databases are robust, secure, responsible (collecting and using only the information necessary for the system´s explicit purpose), and sustainable. Such systems can help encourage open standards and vendor neutrality. They need to help lay down legal and operational principles so that they can establish trust and accountability. Likewise, protecting users' data rights should also feature in these systems (see data-sharing infrastructure below).

In countries where efficient and consistent national ID systems exist, ID could also be used to identify SMEs (Box 7). However, where ID does not exist or is not reliable, alternatives could be considered, such as social security numbers, tax identification numbers, or other ID numbers created in coordination with financial regulators or credit registries.

Data can also be improved by identifying legal entities with a unique, global identifier. This can be a crucial part of efforts to obtain better financial data, especially in support of transactions across borders. The Financial Stability Board (FSB) has published a "Global Legal Entity Identifier" for financial markets,

which sets out 15 global legal entity identifier system high-level principles and 35 recommendations for the development of a unique ID system for parties to financial transactions (FSB n.d.). For larger SMEs, countries should consider adopting a company registration framework or make use of the Legal Entity Identifier provided by the G20 Global Legal Entity System to connect data from different sources to improve the accuracy of linked data. Variants, such as the World Bank's Identification for Development Initiative, could also be considered (World Bank n.d.).

Payment infrastructure

Frequently, firms find their way into digital financial services through digital payments. And digital payment infrastructure is a key initial enabler for advancing the financial inclusion agenda. Inclusive payment infrastructure should result in payment services that can reach any individual or SME. The G20 Policy Guide on Digitalization and informality established some policy guidelines, especially in the context of SMEs operating in the informal economy (Global Partnership for Financial Inclusion and G20 Argentina 2018).

Box 7: Digital Biometric Identification—Expanding Digital Banking in Rural Markets

In Papua New Guinea, a country where some 85% of the low-income population reportedly has no access to formal financial services, the Asian Development Bank's (ADB) digital access tool through biometric ID project is supporting MiBank and Women's Microbank, which provide financial services to low-income and financially underserved people in remote areas.

- The biometric ID allows people to verify personal attributes such as name, gender, and biometrics to access financial services safely and securely. This will aid considerably in establishing know-your-customer information, which is critical to accessing financial services.
- The tool uses smart cards on standard Android mobile phones.
- This smart card-based digital access tool works without power and internet, which is important for reaching unbanked people in the remote locations.

Source: ADB (2019). The Future of Inclusive Finance. Welcome address to the 3rd Asia Finance Forum by Bambang Susantono, ADB Vice-President for Knowledge Management. 6 November. https://www.adb.org/sites/default/files/publication/643831/3rd-asia-finance-forum-conference-proceedings.pdf.

Key parts of the digital payment infrastructure include automated clearing houses, payment switches, and large value and retail payment settlement systems. It also includes certain data sharing and information systems such as credit reporting bureaus and collateral registry systems. In addition, financial institution-level infrastructure, such as core banking systems that could take advantage of cloud technologies, can improve access to digital financial services. Outsourcing services can help payment service providers that face challenges participating directly in key payment infrastructure. In addition, joint payment switches used by banks and nonbanks have been established in several countries (e.g., Malaysia, the Philippines, and Thailand). Infrastructure interoperability between different payment service providers and financial institutions can provide solutions in markets where there is no single joint platform (Box 8).

Ultimately, all retail payment systems need to settle their balances in the respective large value payment systems that operate in central bank money (e.g., real-time gross settlement). These systems are integral in allowing the connection of retail payment systems (including mobile systems), domestically and across borders. In this regard, international standardization of payments and settlement messages should be looked at closely, including ISO 20022 being established and adapted widely in Asia and most parts of the world.[12] The ASEAN Economic Community Blueprint 2025 foresees that all major financial market infrastructure in the region will adopt ISO 20022 by 2025 (ASEAN Secretariat 2015).

Such standardization will facilitate the interoperability of payment systems, especially cross-border, and allow more effective fintech solutions. This will also offer the benefit of greater standard KYC and anti-money laundering approaches, which can be easily applied to domestic as well as cross-border payments (Box 9).

Increasingly, regulators are seeing the potential of interoperable payment systems to support market competition, and achieve greater and more efficient economies of scale using existing infrastructure. Distributed ledger technology (DLT) also offers potential applications that can support greater access to trade and supply chain finance, asset registry systems, and other types of document tracking. New developments and standards for interoperable payments around the use of QR codes have helped increase access to payments for customers and SMEs (Riley 2019).

QR codes in particular have helped several countries leapfrog challenges associated with traditional POS terminals, as only a printed QR code is required and customers just need a smartphone. Additionally, systems that enable fast payments—able to transmit payment

---

Box 8: An Example of an Interoperable Payment System in India

The Unified Payment Interface (UPI), launched by the National Payments Corporation of India in 2016, offers a framework and API-based protocols that allow interoperable retail payments on a mobile platform. UPI supports any source of funds (bank account, prepaid wallet, etc.), and it can be offered by banks directly and nonbanks indirectly (e.g., Google, Amazon). Bank membership in UPI had reached 213 by February, with transactions at over 2.2 billion in the month. The value of transactions in the month was more than $58 billion.

Source: Department of Payment and Settlement Systems of the Reserve Bank of India, with figures based on data from the National Payments Corporation of India.

---

12 For more information see https://www.iso20022.org

Box 9: Indonesia's Digital Payments Regulatory Framework

All banks, mobile network operators, fintech start-ups, Big Tech companies operating digital payments need a license, according to central bank regulations.

Bank Indonesia groups companies into six types—e-money issuer, e-wallet provider, payment gateway operator, merchant acquirer, switching provider, and money remittance/fund transfer operator. All of these have a specific function along the digital payment value chain.

Two types of e-money users are also identified. The "registered" user requires know-your-customer and customer due diligence processes for users by the issuer; "unregistered" users require just name and phone number. It caps balances in e-money accounts at Indonesian rupiah (Rp) 10 million, with monthly maximum transactions limited to Rp20 million for registered users and only Rp2 million for unregistered users. The latter are also only allowed to use services such as e-money transactions. Regulation also defines minimum paid up capital requirements and puts a limit on foreign ownership for firms involved in digital payments.

Source: Indonesia Payment Systems Blueprint 2025. 2019. Jakarta. https://www.bi.go.id/en/publikasi/sistem-pembayaran/riset/Pages/Blueprint-Sistem-Pembayaran-Indonesia-2025.aspx

messages and grant that the availability of funds to the payee occur in real-time or near real-time on a 24/7 basis—may be able to reach substantially higher adoption of digital payments. A fast payments system requires certain activities associated with clearing to occur in real-time or near real-time continuously.

According to the BIS Committee on Payment and Settlement Systems, central banks have a variety of roles, responsibilities, and interests in fostering the safety and efficiency of national payment systems, especially rules governing retail payment systems, services, and payment instruments. More recently, many central banks are also considering accessibility and coverage, effective protection of customers, and existence of a competitive environment as important objectives.

Central banks can adopt one of several roles in retail payments to meet these goals: (i) operational, (ii) as catalyst, and (iii) as overseer or regulator.

In the first role, the central bank generally provides settlement services for one or more retail payment systems. In some countries, it may operate a retail payment system, thus taking a more direct operational role.

In order to discuss priorities for improving payment systems or developing new services and to facilitate such projects, meanwhile, central banks typically maintain close relationships with commercial banks and other payment service providers. In some countries, the monetary authority has established, and usually chairs, a national payment council as a forum for multistakeholder consultations.

As an overseer of payment systems, the central bank's role is focused on the efficiency and safety of the payment system. While this varies from country to country, increasingly, governments have been adopting new national payment systems acts and laws that strengthen their legal and regulatory oversight.

Data-sharing infrastructure

As more individuals and SMEs go online, they create digital footprints with vast amounts of data. Access to this is seen as essential to promote fintech products and services.

Policy makers and regulators are increasingly seeing the importance of providing the right policy-and regulatory-enabling environment to help empower citizens and support use of fintech services increasingly built on the wealth of that data.

While appropriate ID infrastructure is needed to bring the unbanked into the formal financial system, and payment infrastructure can facilitate usage of services, it is data-sharing infrastructure that empowers consumers, businesses, and the broader fintech ecosystem. This key foundational infrastructure requires appropriate data privacy and protection rules to build trust and ensure responsible use of personal and business data.

Countries have taken various approaches to data-sharing policies and regulations. This ranges from market-oriented approaches with little or no regulation to tightly controlled data protection laws such as the GDPR in the European Union. GDPR focuses on preventing harm by shifting the burden for privacy and security to service providers.

Data policy in some countries, however, focuses on making sure that people can best reap the benefits of their data, as in India (BIS 2019b). India's approach has taken a different track from the other approaches to data-sharing infrastructure (such as in the PRC or the EU).

Rather than allow service providers to make use of data without the consent of customers or under strict data privacy rules that focus on penalties for providers, India's approach has been to allow consumers to readily access their data and empower them to decide how to share their data to obtain services, including digital financial services such as credit or insurance (Nilekani 2018).

The Reserve Bank of India, meanwhile, has supported data-sharing infrastructure. The central bank established a legal framework for a class of regulated data fiduciary entities, known as account aggregators. This enables the sharing of data within the regulated financial system with the customer's consent (BIS 2019b). This enabling infrastructure has allowed sharing of data across fintech, banking, investment, insurance, and pension fund sectors. Data to be shared under the framework cover 18 classes of financial information across the banking, investment, insurance, and pension fund sectors.

Policy Environment and Fiscal Incentives

While not necessarily a prerequisite to support the development of fintech, government policies and fiscal incentives can play a key role, especially in attracting entrepreneurs and investors, and providing incentives to support fintech start-ups and promote adoption of fintech services.

Some countries are trying to attract people with fintech skills, as well as investors, using visa programs. This can help countries achieve fintech goals earlier, despite the lengthy process for developing local technical skills and investment.

Many fintech firms, especially start-ups, require access to various funding cycles to grow. While access to capital is limited in emerging markets, governments have provided investment funds alongside the private sector and/or established policies to facilitate foreign investment (Boxes 10 and 11 provide examples of incentives).

Fiscal policies have also included tax incentives such as offering capital gains tax benefits to fintech start-ups or their investors.

Box 10: Singapore's Artificial Intelligence and Data Analytics Grant

The Monetary Authority of Singapore's is offering firms incentive to invest in artificial intelligence (AI).

The country is reimbursing financial and research firms (as much as 50%–70%) for projects tapping the power of AI and data in devising strategy and analyzing business. The $27 million Artificial Intelligence and Data Analytics Grant can encourage use of machine learning, natural language processing, or text analytics, in addition to deep learning or neural networks, and predictive and prescriptive analytics.

Source: Alliance for Financial Inclusion (2020).

Box 11: Australia's Tax Incentives for Start-Ups

In Australia, the Tax Incentive for Early Stage Investors and the New Arrangements for Venture Capital Limited Partnerships are encouraging early investment in start-ups.

The schemes provide a 20% nonrefundable tax offset for qualifying investments—in innovation companies or funds—with a yearly limit of A$200,000 per investor.

Source: Alliance for Financial Inclusion (2020).

ENSURING RESPONSIBLE FINTECH SERVICES

4

Prudential and Market Conduct Regulations

Key messages

Prudential and market conduct rules are the two main approaches to financial regulation.

Prudential regulation is designed to achieve integrity in financial institutions and stable financial systems.

Market conduct regulation aims to protect the consumer from unfair contracting, fraud, and excessive prices, and often supports competition in the marketplace.

Stringent prudential regulations, especially on banks, can ensure a robust and resilient financial system better able to withstand financial instability and systemic risk. To deal with these risks, prudential regulation is targeted at banks well as deposit insurance (Box 12).

The requirements include:

- **Capital requirements.** This refers to how much equity a financial regulator requires of a bank or financial institution, typically in the form of a capital adequacy ratio of equity over risk-weighted assets.
- **Reserve requirements.** This refers to the percentage of assets required to be held as cash, and highly liquid assets that can be used to meet deposit withdrawals and other obligations.
- **Governance requirements.** These are designed to manage financial risks in maturities of deposits and loans, currencies, and other factors relating to the nature of investment.
- **Reporting and disclosure requirements.** These requirements are designed to improve internal governance and external supervision.

However, regulation needs to vary according to the type of financial service and its risk level. Nonetheless, if services are diverse or if only lower-risk financial services are offered, it may not be necessary to provide full banking regulation. Such regulation might prove disproportionate and counterproductive in developing the financial services industry.

Box 12: Fintech and Financial Stability

While fintech is allowing developing Asian economies to leapfrog in this area, concerns exist about possible risks to regional financial stability. Although these emerging firms can broaden financial inclusion, more access to credit might contribute to financial instability if not effectively regulated.

In the People's Republic of China, for example, domestic peer-to-peer (P2P) lending has grown significantly, but along with fraudulent activities amid the lack of regulation. An estimated one-third of all P2P lenders have failed as a result.[a]

Greater reliance on decentralized digital solutions amid financial innovation is also helping to increase operations risk. These include risks of cybersecurity, as well as Anti-Money Laundering and Counter-Terrorism Financing (AML-CTF). Fintech could also encourage financial contagion arising out of new types of financial flows across borders. These would include relatively recent advancements in tokenized securities, blockchain bonds, or cross-border crowdfunding.[b]

In addition, fintech firms are beginning to encroach on the territory of traditional financial service providers. As such, see financial service providers keen to compete to take risks as licenses increasingly fall outside regulatory perimeters. Indeed, regulation and insurance is lacking in fintech and Big Tech companies engaged in deposit and loan businesses, making them akin to shadow banks (Lai and Van Order).[c]

It remains a challenge to regulate fintechs for several reasons: (i) financial regulation remains limited and allows fintech companies to benefit from regulatory arbitrage—and these firms are diversifying into banking and other financial services yet are subject to fewer requirement governing reporting and regulation, with licenses subject to more lax monitoring. In addition, (ii) regulators lack experience in fintechs, which complicates understanding and assessing implications for regulation of these new firms; (iii) many emerging and developing economies suffer significant resource constraints and limit effective responses to fintech risks; and (iv) the focus on the domestic financial landscape raises the risks of cross-border regulatory arbitrage. Regulators have responded with similar innovations as they deal with these emerging risks. Innovation offices and regulatory sandboxes, for example, can help overcome the difficulties of regulatory arbitrage and poor knowledge of fintech activities, with the innovation offices allowing regulators and innovators more opportunity to engage and thus work out viable solutions.

Indeed, greater engagement with fintech firms can boost understanding among regulators of the important trends, risks, and implications for regulation. The resource constraints typical in emerging and developing economies, meanwhile, can be mitigated by encouraging greater regional knowledge-sharing and policy dialogue. This would include venues such as the ASEAN+3 Economic Review and Policy Dialogue.

Developed economies or knowledge-sharing policy platforms, likewise, can guide countries in finding efficient and effective policies and regulations. The coordination inherent to regional knowledge sharing and policy dialogue, meanwhile, may help bring about less regulatory arbitrage by encouraging international best practices for policies and regulations that would produce more standard treatments for companies engage in these practices.

ASEAN+3 = Association of Southeast Asian Nations, the People's Republic of China, Japan and the Republic of Korea.
[a] UN Secretary-General's Special Advocate for Inclusive Finance for Development and CCAF (2019).
[b] IMF. 2019. Fintech: The Experience So Far. https://www.imf.org/en/Publications/Policy-Papers/Issues/2019/06/27/Fintech-The-Experience-So-Far-47056.
[c] Lai, R.N. and R. Van Order. 2017. Fintech Finance and Financial Fragility: Focusing on China. https://papers.ssrn.com/sol3/papers.cfm?abstract_id=3075043.
Source: ADB. 2019. Asian Economic Integration Report 2019/2020. Chapter on Financial Integration. Manila: ADB.

This is particularly true of the fast-evolving fintech market.

For example, some basic financial services do not entail significant systemic risk, and only require certain key protections:

- Conversion of cash to electronic money (cash-in) depends on proper authentication of the cash, identification of the customer, and a reliable bookkeeping system.
- Storage of money for safe keeping depends primarily on the same things, as well as control over access to the funds, making governance, audits, and KYC procedures key to ensuring the integrity of the system.
- Transfers and payment services require documentation of the delivery to and transfer by the network, and authentication of the recipient, and so rely on internal messaging and control protocols to protect against fraud and system failure. Prevention of terrorism finance and money laundering may also justify limiting the amounts that may be transferred, requiring certain record keeping and identification of the sender.

Although these electronic money services may channel money into banking systems, they often only offer money transfer and payment services, meaning that the credit, market, or liquidity risks of full "banking" services are not an issue. Without such risks, there is no need for the prudential regulations that banks face. Instead, market conduct regulation might be enough to provide consumers the protection they need to engender trust. This can be achieved through transparency and disclosure requirements, standards for informing customers of balances held and transactions carried out, and audit requirements. Easier licensing—e.g., electronic money issuer licenses—may therefore be appropriate in most markets.

In alternative nonbank lenders—which have dramatically increased credit to unbanked or underbanked individuals and SMEs, especially when an economy is in an upswing—policy makers and regulators need to be aware that these new lenders and their business models have not faced any stress testing in economic downturns. That is to say, the risks to financial stability during recessions, such as the downturn widely anticipated in the wake of the COVID-19 pandemic, could raise individual and SME delinquency rates.

In addition, regulators and policy makers should adopt principles for responsible innovation and encourage nondiscriminatory access to information to market participants. At the same time, authorities need to stay on top of issues of data fragmentation and the potential for a few large firms to gain monopolistic control over digital data, and thus lock clients into a single service provider.

Fintech and Consumer Protection

Consumer demand and adoption of fintech-enabled services is driven largely by the level of trust and the value proposition of these services. Having effective consumer protection guidelines that also cover the unique issues around fintech can boost trust among consumers and encourage them to use new fintech services.

It has become clear in recent years that through greater consumer protection in financial services, consumers are gaining the ability to make informed financial decisions, exercise rights, and meet obligations. Such safeguards are providing consumer with adequate, timely, and efficient redress for complaints. Regulations in this area thus tend to focus on several related objectives: (i) ensure consumers have information sufficient for more informed financial decisions, (ii) prevent service providers from using unfair practices, and (iii) provide recourse mechanisms to resolve disputes.

In providing these protections, however, authorities should be careful not to place onerous restrictions on the providers, on the financial products they offer, or on the services and delivery channels. These issues become more important when low-income or disadvantaged groups are involved, who may be new to formal financial services and thus vulnerable to unfair practices.

As noted, however, this balancing act places regulators in a dilemma: protecting consumers even as they seek to avoid high compliance costs on fintech providers. High costs risk limiting access to financial services for the target populations and undermining the providing firms' business models. Achieving the right balance will thus mean clearly identifying both the risks and constraints that consumers grapple with, and the language barriers, culture, and general knowledge and attitudes about technology present in the population. Likewise, they will need to understand all issues fintech providers themselves face as they manage the risks and associated extra costs.

In some jurisdictions, regulators have worked closely with the fintech industry to introduce an industry-led code of ethics for responsible fintech services, especially digital credit, that can effectively complement regulatory oversight of the sector. For instance, Indonesia's Financial Services Authority (OJK) has worked with Indonesia's FinTech Lending Association (AFPI) to support and serve as an advocate for responsible fintech lending in the country. More importantly, it aids in the prudential and market conduct monitoring of fintech lending platforms. As part of AFPI, a new code of conduct for responsible lending is being implemented which all fintech lending platforms must follow, and which will be enforced by AFPI with the support of OJK.

Regulators thus need to assess fintech services to identify the vulnerabilities and risks for consumers and SMEs, including direct risks emerging through a mobile phone or other digital channel, or arising through use of a third-party agent or online. Identifying the risks requires measuring impact and its likelihood, which will depend on the environment, types of technology, consumer demand, and factors unique to each market.

Importance of adequate and complete information

Fintech providers should be required to ensure that all their customers have accurate information and terms and conditions about the service, the transactions possible, all transaction fees and rates, transaction limits (if any), and the delivery channels. Clients must also always have access to customer service operators for questions, with information provided in understandable terms in the language they speak daily, whether indigenous or minority languages, not just in the national, financial language.

Other risk factors needing consideration as the regulator prepares consumer protection in fintech services include:

- risks of new technology
- third-party agent risks
- challenges of new services or new fintech providers
- consumer and data privacy concerns, and
- outsourcing to third-party service providers

As regulators set up consumer protection policies and regulations for fintech providers, the following minimum considerations are needed:

- A regulatory framework for consumer protection under a proportionate risk-based approach to prudential standards that also allows innovation and aims overall for financial inclusion.
- Fintech providers are, to the extent possible, licensed to operate under clear rules to guard against misappropriation of consumer funds by the fintech provider, insolvency, fraud, or any operational risk.

- Fintech providers operate on a level and competitive playing field that increases efficiency and consumer choice.
- Appropriate and accurate standards for disclosure and transparency of information.
- Simplified consumer protection rules for low-value transactions guided by the principle of proportionate risk-based policies.
- Fintech providers are responsible for all their services, whether provided directly to consumers or via a third-party or agent.
- Clear data privacy and confidentiality rules that are enforced by the regulator.
- Channels for handling complaints. This includes channels with fintech providers and complaint resolution services externally, via the regulator or a relevant government agency.
- Relevant quantitative and qualitative data is collected to help the regulator fine-tune consumer protection regulation.

Data privacy and protection

Increasing digitalization is deepening the digital footprints that individuals and SMEs leave behind. The use of cloud-based services, financial transactions, making or accepting payments, browsing the internet, the use of mobile apps, interactions in social media, buying or selling online, getting ratings from customers, shipping packages, or online record-keeping are just examples of activities that generate an unprecedented volume of data points that provide increasing opportunities, including access to finance thanks to the use of alternative credit scoring models using advanced analytics. Frequently, many consumers and SMEs will share their data if they think there is value in doing so. But this access to data raises issues about its responsible use and rights to privacy.

While not all countries have defined data privacy laws, several countries are either developing laws or, in the interim, are adopting data privacy regulations under e-commerce or other laws (Box 13).

Many policy makers have introduced regulatory frameworks based on the EU's GDPR of 2016 and enforced in 2018.

The main objective of the GDPR is to give people control of their own personal data and, by unifying regulation in the EU, to create a simpler regulatory environment for international players. The regulation highlights a few important areas:[13]

- No personal data may be processed unless this processing is done under one of six lawful bases specified by the regulation (consent, contract, public task, vital interest, legitimate interest, or legal requirement).
- Business processes that handle personal data must be designed and built with consideration of the principles and provide safeguards to protect data (for example, using pseudonyms or full anonymity where appropriate).
- Data controllers must clearly disclose any data collection, declare the lawful basis and purpose for data processing, and state how long data is being retained and if it is being shared with third parties.

The EU GDPR has become a model for many national laws on data protection and data privacy, such as in the PRC, Japan, the Philippines, and Singapore.

Cybersecurity

Risk to cybersecurity risk is increasing with the expansion of fintech; the growing number of digital transactions; the storage of vast amounts of personal data, and the proliferation of products and services that use or transmit personal identification information or sensitive information (e.g., financial records, account information, tax filling, etc.); and the interconnectivity of more players in the financial system.

New and smaller fintech providers are especially vulnerable to cybersecurity threats, because their security is limited compared to larger financial institutions. In addition, SMEs and individual consumers are especially vulnerable because they may be unaware that their data is valuable to cybercriminals.

In particular, various specific barriers exist for the adoption of cybersecurity by smaller fintechs and SMEs. These barriers generally have to do with limited awareness, the lack of capabilities and resources, the shortage of standards in specific areas, and the lack of clear implementation guidelines. Consideration could be given to publicly sponsored capacity-building initiatives— or co-sponsored by the private sector—aimed at overcoming lack of awareness or insufficient

---

Box 13: Cambodia's Data Privacy Rules Under New Law on E-Commerce

On 8 October 2019, the national assembly approved the Law on Electronic Commerce, establishing several important rules that also apply to fintech-enabled services and electronic payments. The law strengthens the ability to use e-signatures and data privacy. And it features important consumer protection measures, with criminal liability for online harassment and unauthorized uses of personal data privacy, electronic payments and electronic funds transfers, rules for payment service providers, and electronic fraud.

Source: Cambodia Law on Electronic Commerce.

---

[13] See https://gdpr.eu/ for more information on the General Data Protection Regulation.

capacity among smaller fintech providers and SMEs for implementing measures to lower and even prevent cybersecurity risks. These efforts could aim to raise workforce skill levels or otherwise avoid skills becoming obsolete, or give workforces new skills to switch expertise to cybersecurity. They could also involve structural measures that aim to re-educate the upcoming workforce in these areas.

Additionally, authorities could look at efforts to create affordable cybersecurity, particularly programs for smaller fintech providers and SMEs (Box 14). Cooperation and information sharing with national and international agencies, meanwhile, could significantly raise abilities in smaller fintech providers and SMEs to thwart cybersecurity threats.

From a regulatory perspective, a wide range of cybersecurity frameworks exists, yet most are focused nationally or cover a particular sector of the economy. In 2019, the Alliance for Financial Inclusion (AFI) published a report providing key principles and guidelines that help regulatory and supervisory officials create tools for financial sector players to counter cybersecurity risks related to fintech firms and financial institutions. The report outlines the following key principles and guidelines for regulators (AFI 2019):

- Establishing and maintaining a cybersecurity framework to guides fintech firms, financial institutions, and digital solution providers. The framework needs to be of appropriate size for the company in question and the risks its customers face.
- Developing cybersecurity awareness programs for financial service providers, fintech firms, and firms offering digital solutions.
- Ensuring cooperation with the many national agencies that operate in the cybersecurity area and bringing threats and incidents to their attention.
- Where a financial service provider or fintech firm is subject to a cybersecurity failure that causes a data breach or supervisory authorities receive reports of fraud, regulators need to review the cyber threat and bring it to the attention of others also vulnerable to attack.

Box 14: EU Cybersecurity for SMEs

Public-private partnerships in the European Union (EU) are helping small and medium-sized enterprises (SMEs) adopt good practices in tackling cybersecurity risk. For instance, the EU Cybersecurity for SMEs program was founded in 2016 as a collaboration between EU governments, leading technology firms, and academic researchers to help SMEs with cybersecurity issues. The objectives of the program are:

- Develop high-quality cybersecurity solutions for SMEs with a limited budget.
- Provide cybersecurity training and awareness for SMEs and all types of employees.

The cost-effective suite of cybersecurity tools being developed supports SMEs in managing network information security risks and threats, and identifying opportunities to implement secure, innovative technologies.

Source: Digital SME Alliance and European CyberSecurity Organisation (2017).

ASEAN COMPARATIVE FINTECH LAWS, POLICIES, AND REGULATIONS

5

Key messages

Policy initiatives and reforms must be enabled to build the infrastructure for delivery of digital services and to encourage financial institutions to use new digital technology for financial industry development.

New rules or guidelines must be implemented in order to monitor market participants' use of technologies that enable fintech and control for potential risks of technological innovations.

Specific fintech activities should be regulated to protect customers, support anti-money laundering and counter-terrorism financing efforts, and build operational resilience.

As noted in an earlier chapter, three approaches to policies and regulatory environments can support fintech. These include (i) enabling laws and policies, (ii) regulating the technologies that enable fintech, and (iii) regulating specific fintech activities.

The first approach relates to enabling policy initiatives such as those in national identification; data sharing; privacy and protection laws; electronic know-your-customer (e-KYC) polices and regulations; open banking regulations; and innovation hubs, sandboxes, or accelerators.[14] The second approach includes new rules or guidelines on market participants' use of technologies such as cloud computing, artificial intelligence, algorithms, distributed ledger technologies, and Open Application Programming Interfaces. The third approach is about regulating specific fintech activities such as licensing e-money, digital banking, P2P lending, equity crowdfunding, and rules on cryptoassets.

Enabling Fintech Policies

- Most jurisdictions have adopted policies to create the infrastructure for digital services. These include reforms to allow financial institutions to use digital technologies to identify and verify customers without their physical presence.
- In some jurisdictions, such as Malaysia and Singapore, authorities have put in place centralized platforms that provide residents with a unique electronic key that can be used to verify identity in all types of transaction involving both the public and the private sectors.
- Related to digital identification systems, policies and regulations are also being used in biometrics and e-KYC to identify customers in regulated transactions (such as opening a bank account). This is now happening in

---

[14] To complement the innovation office and regulatory sandbox, some financial authorities use structured instruments such as financial accelerators to encourage fintech innovation, while mitigating risks. Accelerators are fixed-term programs that include funding (usually in exchange for equity), mentorship, or education from the sponsoring partners.

Brunei Darussalam, Malaysia, the Philippines, Singapore, and Thailand.[15] Cambodia, the Lao People's Democratic Republic, and Viet Nam are all piloting digital national ID systems.

- Malaysia and Singapore have also moved to regulate the exchange of customer information between different players, and the Philippines has developed strict policies for data privacy and protection under its National Privacy Commission.
- In addition, most advanced and emerging market economies have set up various arrangements to promote orderly application of new technologies in the financial industry. These arrangements include innovation hubs, regulatory sandboxes, and accelerators. Brunei Darussalam, Indonesia, Malaysia, the Philippines, Singapore, and Thailand have supported these types of enabling regulatory approaches.
- In another policy approach, initially promoted in the European Union under the Revised Payment Services Directive, regulators aim to drive increased competition and innovation by opening up customer banking data to third parties via open banking regulations. Open banking initiatives focused on working with the private sector to develop standards are now also happening in Indonesia, Malaysia, the Philippines, and Singapore.
- Innovation hubs are the most widespread of these facilitators. Such hubs support and guide fintech providers to facilitate better understanding of regulatory requirements. Several jurisdictions have also created test-and-learn approaches or use regulatory sandboxes that allow assessment of the risks associated with new business models in a controlled environment. So far, test-and-learn approaches (initiated in the

Philippines) and regulatory sandboxes in Malaysia, Singapore, and Thailand have been used mainly to assess whether consumers would be adequately protected while using new applications, products, or services. Approaches vary on criteria for accepting projects, testing parameters, application processes, and exit strategies. In some cases, the final outcome is simply an authorization to continue offering the tested products or services, while in others it may also include an adjustment or a formal clarification of existing regulatory requirements. However, financial regulators should be cautious about too much direct involvement in supporting individual fintech firms or services to avoid conflict of interest. Almost all ASEAN regulators have active innovation hubs and regulatory sandboxes (Figure 2).

Regulating the Use of Enabling Technologies

- Several jurisdictions have moved to address both the positive implications and the risks of specific innovations. Supporting policies include those to facilitate the use of open application programming interfaces, explicitly promoted for open banking. Singapore especially has employed these, with standards for their use likewise now being developed in Indonesia, Malaysia, and the Philippines.
- In distributed ledger technology, regulators in Malaysia and Singapore are taking action to provide legal certainty for this technology for settlement of transactions, especially in the use of smart contracts.[16]
- Malaysia, the Philippines, Singapore, and Thailand have also allowed banks and other regulated financial institutions to use cloud

---

[15] For further information see P. Bhunia. 2018. MAS Issues Guidance to Allow Use of Innovative Solutions for Customer On-Boarding. https://www.opengovasia.com/mas-issues-guidance-to-allow-use-of-innovative-technology-solutions-for-customer-on-boarding/; as well BNM. 2019. Electronic Know-Your-Customer (e-KYC): Exposure Draft. https://www.bnm.gov.my/index.php?ch=57&pg=543&ac=867&bb=file; and S. Banchongduang. 2020. BoC Carves out KYC Path for Banking. Bangkok Post. 8 February. https://www.bangkokpost.com/business/1853114/bot-carves-out-e-kyc-path-for-banking.

[16] For more information on these efforts see (i) the Monetary Authority of Singapore's Blockchain/Distributed Ledger Technology at https://www.mas.gov.sg/development/fintech/technologies---blockchain-and-dlt; (ii) MyGovernment at https://www.malaysia.gov.my/portal/content/30633; and Hong Kong Monetary Authority. Distributed Ledger Technology at https://www.hkma.gov.hk/eng/key-functions/international-financial-centre/fintech/research-and-applications/distributed-ledger-technology-dlt/

Figure 6: Regulatory Sandbox Initiatives Across ASEAN

Operational sandbox
- Thailand
- Malaysia
- Singapore
- Brunei Darussalam
- Philippines
- Indonesia

Proposed sandbox
- Viet Nam

ASEAN = Association of Southeast Asian Nations.
Source: UNSGSA FinTech Working Group and CCAF. Early Lessons on Regulatory Innovations to Enable Inclusive Fintech (2019) and CCAF (2019).

computing, with specific recommendations to control and manage technology risks.[17]

- In addition, some authorities are addressing the risks of misuse of artificial intelligence and machine learning algorithms, for instance, in credit or insurance underwriting. The Monetary Authority of Singapore has published guidance listing underlying risks arising from the inadequate handling of personal data, poor governance, lack of transparency, and unethical behavior. The authority has also issued high-level principles for firms to follow.

Regulating Specific Fintech Activities

- Banking licenses are still required to conduct any activity entailing substantial risk related to converting funds raised from the public.

However, when nonbank financial institutions are allowed to source cash from the public— typically for payment services—they face restrictions for safeguarding customers' funds. Examples include maximum volumes or ample liquidity coverage, such as the 100% reserve requirements for outstanding client balances (the float) in most countries, including all countries in ASEAN, except for the Lao People's Democratic Republic and Brunei Darussalam.

- Digital banking is a relatively new area, with rapid developments across ASEAN, especially in Malaysia, the Philippines, and Singapore.[18]
- Specific licensing and conduct-of-business requirements have been established for activities such as issuance of e-money; provision of payment services, equity crowdfunding, P2P, marketplace lending;

[17] For more information on these efforts see the Monetary Authority of Singapore's Cloud at https://www.mas.gov.sg/development/fintech/technologies---cloud; Bank Negara Malaysia's Risk Management in Technology at https://www.bnm.gov.my/documents/20124/963937/Risk+Management+in+Technology+(RMiT).pdf/810b088e-6f4f-aa35-b603-1208ace33619?t=1592866162078; and Bangko Sentral ng Pilipinas' Enhanced Guidelines on Information Security Management at https://www.bsp.gov.ph/Regulations/Issuances/2017/c982.pdf; For the Bank of Thailand effort, see Regulations on IT Outsourcing for Business Operations of Financial Institutions at https://www.bot.or.th/Thai/FIPCS/Documents/FPG/2560/EngPDF/25600035.pdf.
[18] For more information about each country's efforts see (i) Bank Negara Malaysia's 2020 document, Licensing Framework for Digital Bank: Exposure Draft at https://www.bnm.gov.my/documents/20124/938039/20201231_Licensing+Framework+for+Digital+Banks.pdf; (ii) Bangko Sentral ng Pilipinas 2020 Guidelines on the Establishment of Digital Banks at https://www.bsp.gov.ph/Regulations/Issuances/2020/c1105.pdf; and (iii) the Monetary Authority of Singapore's 2018 document, Eligibility Criteria and Requirements for Digital Banks, at https://www.mas.gov.sg/-/media/Digital-Bank-Licence/Eligibility-Criteria-and-Requirements-for-Digital-Banks.pdf.

and the use of bank and nonbank agents, especially across Indonesia and Malaysia.[19] In most cases, regulatory requirements focus on consumer and investor protection, in particular the safeguarding of customers' funds, anti-money laundering, and combating the financing of terrorism, and operational resilience.

- Regulations on crypto assets and now virtual assets differ markedly across jurisdictions. However, new FATF guidance is not quite clear and will be enforced. All jurisdictions that allow, virtual assets, including crypto asset exchanges, to operate will need to register or license them and actively supervise and monitor them.[20] Use of virtual assets has increased in Malaysia, the Philippines, Singapore, and Thailand, especially initial coin offerings. Regulators have had to introduce bespoke regulation or retrofit current regulation to oversee these activities and to now be compliant with new FATF guidance. New supervisory tools (suptech) that allow for the monitoring of crypto exchanges are being actively deployed by regulators in all markets that allow these exchanges to operate.

Globally, fintech policies have also aimed to minimize the scope for regulatory arbitrage. This is especially important in markets with multiple financial regulatory agencies. Most policy makers recognize that new technologies can help new players perform activities traditionally only conducted by tightly regulated institutions. Fintech regulation should therefore be adjusted to prevent firms from "migrating" their risk-generating business activities between regulatory authorities in search of lighter regulatory controls. The concept "same activity, same regulation"— a regulated activity should be subject to the same rules, regardless of nature or legal status—is often seen as a reference for sound policy to promote equal treatment and prevent regulatory arbitrage as fintech firms emerge, especially Big Tech.

---

[19] For information, see the Consultative Group to Assist the Poor, The Use of Agents by Digital Financial Services Providers, at https://www.cgap.org/research/publication/use-agents-digital-financial-services-providers

[20] See Updated Guidance for Risk-Based Approach for Virtual Assets and Virtual Asset Service Providers, FATF 28 Oct 2021 https://www.fatf-gafi.org/publications/fatfrecommendations/documents/guidance-rba-virtual-assets-2021.html

ASEAN Comparative Fintech Laws/Policies/Regulations

	Licensing e-Money	Digital banking	Open banking	P2P and marketplace lending	Equity crowdfunding	Cryptoassets	Open application programming interfaces	Distributed ledger technology	e-KYC	Cloud computing	Artificial intelligence and algorithms	National ID	Data sharing, privacy, and protection	Innovation hubs, accelerators, and regulatory sandboxes
Brunei Darussalam	Green	Orange	Yellow	Green	Green	Orange	Yellow	Yellow	Green	Orange	Orange	Yellow	Yellow	Green
Cambodia	Green	Orange	Orange	Yellow	Orange	Orange	Orange	Yellow	Yellow	Yellow	Orange	Yellow	Orange	Yellow
Indonesia	Green	Green	Yellow	Green	Green	Yellow	Yellow	Yellow	Yellow	Yellow	Yellow	Yellow	Yellow	Green
Lao PDR	Orange	Orange	Orange	Orange	Orange	Orange	Orange	Orange	Yellow	Orange	Orange	Yellow	Orange	Yellow
Malaysia	Green	Green	Green	Green	Green	Green	Green	Green	Green	Green	Green	Green	Green	Green
Philippines	Green	Green	Green	Yellow	Green	Green	Yellow	Yellow	Green	Green	Orange	Yellow	Green	Green
Singapore	Green	Green	Green	Green	Green	Green	Green	Green	Green	Green	Green	Green	Green	Green
Thailand	Green	Green	Orange	Green	Yellow	Green	Orange	Green	Green	Green	Green	Yellow	Green	Green
Viet Nam	Green	Green	Yellow	Yellow	Yellow	Orange	Yellow	Yellow	Yellow	Yellow	Yellow	Yellow	Yellow	Yellow

● (Green) Current law/regulation or policy in place

● (Yellow) Law/regulation or policy being developed or planned

● (Orange) No law/regulation or policy in place

ASEAN = Association of Southeast Asian Nations, ID = identification, KYC = know-your-customer, Lao PDR = Lao People's Democratic Republic, P2P = peer-to-peer.

CONCLUSION AND RECOMMENDATIONS

Digital financial services (fintech) are increasingly beneficial to individual users, governments, and businesses and can be especially useful in broadening inclusive economic growth. Indeed, the COVID-19 pandemic has raised the urgency of their use as economic lockdowns have threatened to undo recent progress in this latter area.

However, responsible and inclusive digital finance ecosystems require the right mix of enabling policies and regulations that ensure safety and soundness principles. Such an environment can also help countries in their efforts to meet the Sustainable Development Goals.

The following eight policy recommendations can help encourage digital financial services that are developing in different ways and speeds across Asia and the Pacific. These trends and tools can help policy makers and regulators harness the emerging services while ensuring safety and soundness.

Legal and Regulatory Framework

Ensuring an appropriate and enabling legal and regulatory framework is crucial for an environment that supports development and use of responsible fintech services. The framework must both identify obstacles to innovation and adapt to new risks. Legal frameworks should provide legal predictability to support investment and ensure that consumers' rights are protected, as well as a legal basis for smart contracts and electronic signatures.

Build Regulatory/Supervisory Capacity

Given the challenges of new technologies and digital financial service providers, regulatory and supervisory capacity must be continually enhanced. Many regulators have developed innovative approaches to better understand and monitor fintech development. These include innovation offices, test-and-learn approaches to regulation, and regulatory sandboxes. A suitable framework also ensures appropriate

legal authorization to supervise fintech service providers and take corrective actions to address safety and soundness concerns. Legal frameworks should also provide legal protection for supervisors. Supervisory departments should regularly evaluate staffing requirements and existing staff skills and take measures to bridge gaps. Supervising fintech providers also requires new approaches and tools, including regulatory technologies (regtech) and supervisory technologies (suptech).

Foundational Infrastructure

Policy makers need to understand the role and level of development of the foundational infrastructure in their own markets and address the gaps. The three essential foundational elements include identification, digital payments, and data-sharing infrastructure.

(i) Identification infrastructure focuses on developing safe, secure, and accessible national digital identification systems that support biometric and e-KYC. International standards for digital national ID systems should be considered as countries develop this critical infrastructure.

(ii) Digital payments are often the entry point for digital financial services. Inclusive payment infrastructure should result in payment services that can reach any individual or SME. Digital payment infrastructure includes automated clearinghouses, payment switches, and large value and retail payment settlement systems. It also contains certain data sharing and information systems, such as credit reporting bureaus and collateral registry systems. Also, financial-institution-level infrastructure, such as core-banking systems that could take advantage of cloud technologies, can broaden access to digital financial services.

(iii) As individuals and businesses expand the use of digital channels, they create substantial amounts of data that can be used to provide access to fintech products and services. Data-sharing infrastructure can broaden the range of financial services as well as empower consumers and businesses, with appropriate data privacy and protection rules to build trust and the responsible use of data.

Main Approaches to Regulating Fintech

Regulators need to follow the latest developments that promote fintech-enabled financial services, including understanding the three main regulatory approaches: fintech enabling laws and policies, regulating enabling technologies, and regulating specific fintech activities.

Prudential and Market Conduct

Understand the critical aspects of prudential and market conduct regulatory approaches for digital finance. To protect the stability of the financial system, regulators need to treat similar risks equally; apply laws and regulations proportionately; avoid market concentration and unfair practices; and foster standardization, interoperability, and interconnectivity in a safe manner.

Digital Financial Literacy

Support digital financial awareness and literacy by embedding digital finance in national financial inclusion and literacy strategies. Establishing trust, safety, and security is crucial if clients are to adopt fintech-enabled financial services.

Competition and Coordination

Policy makers and regulators need to support competition, inter-regulatory coordination, and public and private dialogue. Cooperation and coordination among regulators and supervisors are also essential in supporting an effective regulatory and supervisory framework for all financial institutions, including new fintech providers or third-party service providers. Regulatory and supervisory responsibilities must be delineated and coordinated to avoid regulatory arbitrage. Coordination and consultation with other regulators can help ease providers' regulatory burdens and thus keep compliance costs down. Close coordination and regular dialogue with fintech sector players will also allow regulators to better support regulatory responses.

Safeguard Integrity

Effective consumer protection guidelines covering the unique issues around fintech can help build consumer trust and confidence, which can improve uptake and usage. These include ensuring that providers are fully transparent with consumers, that market conduct rules are in place to prevent unfair practices, and that appropriate redress mechanisms exist. Consumer protection regulations tend to pursue the following broad objectives:

(i)   Ensure consumers have enough information to make informed financial decisions.
(ii) Prevent unfair practices by service providers.
(iii) Ensure consumers have access to recourse mechanisms to resolve disputes.

Safeguarding consumers in the digital age also requires specific measures to ensure cybersecurity, data privacy, and protection. This includes mitigating the risks of money laundering and financing of terrorism that new fintech products and services, especially cryptoassets, may pose.

ANNEX 1: LIST OF DEFINITIONS

Digital payments	These are, technically, payments made using digital instruments wherein the payer and the payee both use electronic modes to send and receive money.[1]
Electronic money (e-money)	This is, broadly, an electronic store of monetary value on a technical device that may be widely used for making payments to entities other than the e-money issuer. The device acts as a prepaid bearer instrument which does not necessarily involve bank accounts in transactions.[2]
Personal financial management and digital financial literacy tools	Personal financial management software can, among other functions, allow categorization of transactions and sorting of accounts from several institutions into a single view on a device. It can also present such things as spending trends, budgets, or net worth as "data visualizations."[3] In several markets, digital financial tools not only offer lessons about digital finance, but also provide simple personal financial management tools such as reminders about savings targets or responsible credit practices.
Digital savings products and services	These commonly refer to digitally accessible interest-bearing deposit accounts held at regulated deposit-taking institutions. However, while all digital savings accounts are ultimately held by regulated deposit-taking institutions, collectively, they may be facilitated by or pass through nonbank fintech providers. These are usually differentiated from e-money and other basic store-of-value accounts. Digital savings accounts and digital store-of-value accounts differ mainly in that the former seeks to explicitly incentivize saving by offering a contractually specified financial return and compensating customers for the time-value of money. As such, digital savings accounts help customers build wealth and save for the long term (World Bank 2019a).
Digital banking	Broadly, this is the application of technology to various banking products, services, and processes, making the customer's experience simple and convenient, and eliminating the need to transact at a physical bank branch (Techfunnel 2020). Digital banking includes categories of new virtual banks with full banking licenses: "neo banks" without a banking license but partnered with a financial institution to offer bank-licensed services (such as WeBank by Tencent in the People's Republic of China [PRC]); and "beta banks," which are joint ventures or subsidiaries of existing banks that offer full digital banking services (such as AiBank, a joint venture between the PRC's CITIC Bank Corp and Baidu). Digital banking models also include partnerships between banks and mobile network operators[4] and third-party providers.[5]

---

[1] Also see the definitions used by the Better Than Cash Alliance and the Committee on Payments and Settlements at https://www.betterthancash.org/tools-research/toolkits/payments-measurement/focusing-your-measurement/introduction.

[2] See definition at European Central Bank n.d. Electronic Money. https://www.ecb.europa.eu/stats/money_credit_banking/electronic_money/html/index.en.html.

[3] For more information see https://www.investopedia.com/personal-financial-management-pfm-5181311.

[4] See the Commercial Bank of Africa's M-Shwari Kenya at https://equitygroupholdings.com/ke/about-equity and M-Pawa in Tanzania and https://vcdacom.co.tz/.

[5] For example, the partnership between Fidelity Bank, Tiaxa, and Airtel in Ghana https://airtel.africa/media/ghana-partners-fidelity-bank, and the MyBucks partnership models with Opportunity Bank in Uganda and Mozambique, http://corporate.mybucks.com/partnership.

Credit scoring and data analytics	These involve a range of new models, including third-party fintech service providers that help credit providers use data analysis to improve credit scores. A credit scoring model is a risk management tool that assesses the creditworthiness of a loan applicant by estimating the probability of default based on historical data. It uses numerical tools to rank cases using multiple sources of data integrated into a single value that attempts to measure risk or creditworthiness.[6]
Insurtech	Insurance technology refers largely to technological innovations that can produce cost savings and greater efficiency in insurance offerings. It also includes the introduction of new fintech-enabled insurance providers such as Slice, Lemonade, and Hippo, which target different customer segments with instant mobile access to insurance.
Crypto and virtual assets	The Bank for International Settlements (BIS) defines these as assets with value determined by supply and demand, similar in concept to commodities such as gold. But in contrast to commodities, they have zero intrinsic value. Unlike traditional e-money, they are neither a liability of any individual or institution nor are they backed by any authority. As a result, their value relies only on the belief that they might later be exchanged for other goods or services or a certain amount of sovereign currency.

The establishment or creation of new units (i.e., the management of total supply), is typically determined by a computer protocol. In those cases, no single entity has the discretion to manage the supply of units over time—instead, this is often determined by an algorithm.

FATF further defines virtual assets as a digital representation of value that can be digitally traded or transferred. Virtual assets can be used for investment or payment. In addition, virtual asset service providers or business that exchange virtual assets for fiat currencies or other virtual assets, facilitate virtual asset transfers, safeguard or administer viral assets, or those that participate in the provision of financial services related to the sale or issuance of a virtual asset.

Different schemes have different long-run supplies and different predetermined rules for the creation and issuance of new units. These predetermined rules help create scarcity in supply. These schemes tend not to be denominated in or tied to a sovereign currency, such as the US dollar or the euro. Using Bitcoin as an example, a bitcoin is the unit of value   that is transferred.

The second distinguishing feature of these schemes is the way in which value is transferred from a payer to a payee. Until recently, a peer-to-peer exchange between parties to a transaction in the absence of trusted intermediaries was typically restricted to money in a physical format. electronic representations of money are usually exchanged in centralized infrastructure, where a trusted entity clears and settles transactions. |

---

[6]   For information about credit scoring, see the Consultative Group to Assist the Poor's (CGAP) Technical Guide at https://www.cgap.org/sites/default/files/publications/2019_07_Technical_Guide_CreditScore.pdf.

The key innovation of some of these virtual asset schemes is the use of distributed ledgers to allow remote P2P exchanges of electronic value in the absence of trust between the parties and without the need for intermediaries. Typically, in a digital wallet, a payer stores cryptographic keys that give access to the value. The payer then uses these keys to initiate a transaction that transfers a specific amount of value to the payee. That transaction then goes through a confirmation process that validates the transaction and adds it to a unified ledger, of which many copies are distributed across the P2P network. Confirmation for virtual asset schemes can vary in speed, efficiency, and security. In effect, distributed ledgers replicate the P2P exchange of value, although on a remote basis over the internet.

Closely related to how value is transferred is the way in which transactions are recorded and in which value is stored. As mentioned above, the transfer is completed when the ledger that is distributed across the decentralized network is updated. The amount of information stored in the ledger can vary from a bare minimum—such that the identity of payers and payees is difficult to ascertain and only the distribution of value across network nodes is kept—to a wealth of information that can include details about the payer, payee, transactions, and balances. In many cases today, digital currency schemes require very little information to be kept in the ledger.

Another distinguishing feature of these schemes is their institutional arrangements. In traditional e-money schemes, several service providers are essential to or embedded in the operation of an e-money scheme: the issuers of e-money, the network operators, the vendors of specialized hardware and software, the acquirers of e-money, and the clearer(s) of e-money transactions.

In contrast, many virtual asset schemes are not operated by any specific individual or institution (though some are promoted actively by certain intermediaries). This differs from traditional e-money schemes that have one or more issuers of value that represent liabilities on the issuers' balance sheets.

Moreover, the decentralized nature of some digital currency schemes means that there is no identifiable scheme operator, a role that is typically played by financial institutions or other institutions that specialize in clearing in the case of e-money. However, a number of intermediaries supply various technical services. These intermediaries may provide "wallet" services to enable users of the virtual asset to transfer value or may offer services to facilitate the exchange between virtual asset units and sovereign currencies, other virtual currency units, or other assets. In some instances, these intermediaries store the cryptographic keys to the value for their customers.[7]

---

[7] This definition of digital currencies draws largely from the BIS definition. Please see BIS (2015a).

A notable variation of private virtual crypto assets is "stablecoins." As the name might imply, such crypto assets aim to minimize price volatility relative to a designated "stable" asset or basket of assets. Thus, stablecoins may be pegged to a, fiat money or exchange-traded commodities (precious or industrial metals, for example).[8] As the BIS and the Group of Seven countries note, however, significant risks are associated with such schemes. These can include legal, financial, operational, or compliance risks concerning money laundering and terrorist financing. They can also include competition law, and consumer and investor protection (BIS 2020a).

Central bank digital currency

Often referred to as digital fiat currency (International Telecommunication Union 2017), this is the digital form of fiat money (a currency established as money by government regulation, monetary authority, or law). Central bank digital currency is different from virtual currency and cryptocurrency, which are not issued by the state and lack the legal tender status declared by the government. Central bank digital currency promises to provide cash-like safety and convenience for P2P payments. However, the challenge in design has been to ensure resilience and accessibility, while safeguarding the user's privacy and allowing effective law enforcement (Auer and Böhme 2020).

Digital accounting and business tool providers

These involve a range of fintech firms offering digital accounting and business tools that help support the digitization of SMEs.

Meanwhile, there are several *alternative digital finance* providers. These include:

(i)   Marketplace platforms
    a. institutional balance sheet lenders
    b. P2P lending models
    c. equity-based crowdfunding.
(ii) Big Tech lenders often connected to e-commerce/payment platforms.
(iii) Supply chain and trade finance platforms

(i)   Marketplace platforms

These lending and financing models include nonbank platform providers which originate loans to clients through intermediary digital platforms[9] and that connect borrowers to individual or institutional lenders. This broad category includes P2P lending platforms, online balance sheet lenders, and equity crowdfunding platforms. There are also nonbank marketplaces for debt and real estate sales, as well as trading nonperforming loans.

---

8   For information, see https://www.investopedia.com/terms/s/stablecoin.asp#:~:text=Stablecoins%20are%20cryptocurrencies%20that%20attempt,commodity's%20price%20such%20as%20gold and https://news.bitcoin.com/more-than-77-crypto-projects-claim-to-be-backed-by-physical-gold/.

9   Digital platforms used by marketplace lenders are increasingly being accessed primarily via the mobile channel in emerging markets while still being available via computer in more developed markets.

P2P lending models. Using such platforms, borrowers can source loans, largely from individual or institutional investors. However, both borrowers and lenders are customers of the platform, each with their own risks, that present challenges in that development of regulation for these lending models is only beginning in Asia. While P2P models started in the UK, the US, and the PRC, these models are now expanding in South and Southeast Asia, especially in India and Indonesia, where regulatory developments are attempting to catch up with the rapid growth in P2P and other alternative finance and credit providers (Cambridge Centre for Alternative Finance 2018a; BIS 2018).

In the PRC, as well as other emerging markets, P2P lending platforms have utilized a hybrid offline-to-online approach to sourcing client data, such as collecting e-commerce transactions and digital payments, as well as analyzing online search histories and social media data. These platforms complement online alternative data with offline credit and background checks by partnering with nonbank financial institutions or by leveraging the platform's own agents or staff to visit the borrower's business to verify their information (for example, by taking pictures of the workplace).

Online balance sheet lenders. These differ from P2P lenders since they retain their own portfolios and collect interest over the life of the loan portfolio. In addition—unlike P2P lending where investors only earn interest once they are matched with a borrower—for balance sheet lenders, the funds are pooled, and interest starts accumulating immediately. Balance sheet lenders can offer lower risk for investors since the online balance sheet lender's capital acts as the "first loss" buffer for investors.[10]

Many online balance sheet lenders focus on specialized market niches like merchant cash advances or point-of-sale financing. Risks associated with online balance sheet lenders are generally easier to manage, since there is usually one key lender and the main credit provider controls all aspects of the lending, unlike P2P lenders, where multiple parties may be involved.

Banks are increasingly teaming up with marketplace lenders (both P2P and online balance sheet lenders) or launching their own platforms as a way to facilitate clients, especially SME clients that they initially deem too risky based on the lack of a credit or business history.

Examples include Beehive by Belgasprombank in Belarus and Credits for Ukrainian Business launched by PrivatBank in Ukraine. The latter makes it possible for SMEs to borrow from the bank's clients, with PrivatBank facilitating disbursements and collections. However, because many small investors did not understand the risks, especially that their investments were not guaranteed, the bank discontinued this service in 2017. Examples such as this provide early lessons for regulators in other markets to ensure that small investors are appropriately warned and protected.

---

[10] H. Swersky. 2015. P2P and Balance Sheet Lending: Same but Different… *Finance Magnates*. 28 December. https://www.financemagnates.com/FinTech/bloggers/p2p-and-balance-sheet-lending-same-same-but-different/.

Two specific subcategories of balance sheet lenders that often raise consumer protection challenges include mobile nano lending providers and digital payday lenders. Mobile nano lenders focus mostly on consumer lending and offer very small loans utilizing credit scoring models based on mobile transaction history, mobile e-money usage, credit history, location data and/ or text data. Many of these mobile-based lenders use data from apps running on smartphones that upload short messaging service (SMS) messages, emails, metadata from calls, tracking geo-locational data of the users, as well as access to social media accounts.

For mobile lenders, such as Tala, even data such as battery recharge frequency, number of incoming text messages, miles traveled in a day, whether a client gambles, or even how the client enters contact names into the phone (such as entering a last name), can be utilized as alternative data for credit scoring (Dwoskin 2015). Under this specific subcategory, regulators have raised specific concerns about data privacy, and countries such as the Philippines have had to deal with numerous cases of abuse (National Privacy Commission 2019).

The other subcategory of specific concern is digital payday lenders, which include a number of salary-based lenders that have shifted to online (mostly mobile) platform delivery models.[11] As with traditional payday lenders, digital payday lenders focus primarily on salary workers, but they also make use of alternative data for credit scoring. The speed and ease of digital lending, along with digital push-marketing techniques, have raised concerns about over-indebtedness, especially for low-income salary workers who have become dependent on this category of digital lender in some markets. Unclear data usage and abusive collection practices have also been a major concern of this category of lender in some markets (Kaushik 2019).

Equity-based crowdfunding platforms. These allow individual and institutional investors to invest in unlisted small and especially medium enterprises in exchange for shares. By definition, equity crowdfunding serves funding of legal entities that can raise funds by selling their equity. It is particularly suitable for start-ups and SMEs. The platform charges a commission based on the amount raised and, in some cases, on the basis of future profit.[12]

The objective of the equity crowdfunding platforms is to provide transparent information to the investors so that they can evaluate the potential investment opportunity. Similar to P2P lending business models, investors are able to make investments in multiple companies in equity-based crowdfunding, diversifying their risk. Equity-based crowdfunding allows companies to raise capital to invest in their companies through alternative channels. These may be a lot easier and cheaper than trying to raise capital from private investors. Retail investors also have an opportunity to generate significant returns if they bet on a new start-up that becomes the next market leader.

---

[11] See Chao (2017); Also see *Quartz* on Paylater in Nigeria at https://qz.com/africa/1568373/dozies-paylater-to-convert-to-digital-bank/.

[12] For more information, see the CGAP working paper at https://www.cgap.org/sites/default/files/Working-Paper-Crowdfunding-and-Financial-Inclusion-Mar-2017.pdf.

(ii) **Big Tech** lenders include subsidiaries of e-commerce, search, payments, and social networking technology companies leveraging their large user bases and access to client data, either directly or via partnerships, to offer digital credit. These companies include Alibaba, Tencent, Baidu, DHgate.com in the PRC; Amazon India, Flipkart, Lendingart, NeoGrowth in India; and now several multicountry cross-border lending models in other regions, such as Southeast Asia. While most of these providers focus on easing credit access for their customer bases, they also tightly control client data, making it harder for others to access.

Debt capacity for most credit customers who sell on e-commerce sites is determined primarily from sales history without a broader understanding of an individual's credit history or overall financial picture. However, e-commerce providers that offer digital credit to those who sell on their platforms, and then automatically deduct repayments from future online sales, have maintained high repayment rates.

(iii) **Supply chain and trade finance platforms** support SME financing focused on purchase orders, invoices, receivables, and pre- and post-shipment processes between buyers and sellers along the supply chain. Cloud-based digital supply chain platforms gain insights into complex trade flows by digitizing documents and transactions and applying data analytics to make credit decisions. They also leverage the financial stability and strength of bond-rated large corporations (often large department store chains or manufacturers) buying SME products or services to offer faster and cheaper SME financing.

These platforms vary widely (e.g., invoice or receivables discounting, payables financing, dynamic discounting, working capital auctions, factoring, inventory finance, pre-shipment finance, etc.), as do their funding sources (e.g., banks, investors, corporate buyers, lenders, etc.). For all, digitization provides more efficient SME lending for suppliers, accelerates approval, increases SME credit access, reduces the chance of supplier or procurement fraud, and sometimes lowers the cost of financing for SMEs. Noteworthy examples include Kickfurther, Tungsten, Basware, Tradeshift, and Kinara Capital. Many of these models work by digitizing the value chain, allowing for innovations such as contracts that trigger immediate payments and loan disbursements when they are delivered and scanned. Open supply chain models where different providers may compete for customers appear to have fewer consumer protection issues, given the competition in their niche markets and relative sophistication of their clients. Issues arise in some older models where banks linked to large companies have locked in customers seeking credit advances by tightly controlling a client's sales data (Owens 2018).

Distributed ledger technology has the potential to enhance trade finance (World Economic Forum and Bain & Company 2018). Smart contracts can improve efficiency and transparency. The technology can allow real-time review of financial documents and bills of lading, helping to reduce counterparty risk. More importantly, smart contracts facilitated by digital ledger technology could eliminate the need for correspondent banks and additional transaction fees. In addition, utilizing a digital platform to track trade finance deals creates a data pool about potential clients and their transaction histories, which could make it easier for fintech firms to offer financing options.

ANNEX 2: ASEAN COMPARATIVE FINTECH LAWS, POLICIES, AND REGULATIONS

ASEAN Comparative Fintech Laws, Policies, and Regulations

	Licensing e-Money	Digital banking	Open banking	P2P and marketplace lending	Equity crowdfunding	Cryptoassets	Open APIs	Distributed ledger technology	e-KYC	Cloud computing	Artificial intelligence and algorithms	National ID	Data sharing, privacy, and protection	Innovation hubs, accelerators, and regulatory sandboxes
Brunei Darussalam	green	orange	yellow	green	green	orange	yellow	yellow	green	orange	orange	yellow	yellow	green
Cambodia	green	orange	orange	yellow	orange	orange	orange	yellow	yellow	yellow	orange	yellow	yellow	yellow
Indonesia	green	green	yellow	green	green	green	yellow	yellow	green	yellow	yellow	green	green	green
Lao PDR	orange	orange	orange	orange	orange	orange	orange	orange	yellow	orange	orange	yellow	orange	yellow
Malaysia	green	green	green	green	green	green	green	green	green	green	green	green	green	green
Philippines	green	green	yellow	green	yellow	yellow	yellow	green	green	green	orange	yellow	green	green
Singapore	green	green	green	green	green	green	green	green	green	green	green	green	green	green
Thailand	green	green	yellow	green	yellow	green	yellow	green	green	green	green	yellow	green	green
Viet Nam	green	green	yellow	yellow	yellow	orange	yellow	yellow	green	yellow	yellow	yellow	green	yellow

- green — Current law/regulation or policy in place
- yellow — Law/regulation or policy being developed or planned
- orange — No law/regulation or policy in place

API = application programming interface, ASEAN = Association of Southeast Asian Nations, ID = identification, KYC = know-your-customer, Lao PDR = Lao People's Democratic Republic, P2P = peer-to-peer.

Brunei Darussalam

Licensing e-money: e-money is regulated under Notice No. PSO/B-1?2020/1 – Amendment No. 1 Requirement for Payment Systems.[a]

Digital banking: No regulations.

Open banking: No Regulations.

Peer-to-peer and marketplace lending: Autoriti Monetari Brunei Darussalam (AMBD) introduced Notice No. CMA/N-1/2019/13 for Peer-to-Peer Platform Operators.

Equity crowdfunding: AMBD issued a notice on equity crowdfunding platform operators on 10 August 2017.

Cryptoassets: No regulations.

Open application programming interface (API): No regulations.

Distributed ledger technology: No regulations.

Electronic know-your-customer (e-KYC): No regulations.

Cloud computing: No regulations.

Artificial intelligence: No regulations.

National digital identification (ID) enabling financial services: No regulations.

Data sharing, privacy, and protection: No regulations.

Innovation hubs, accelerators, and regulatory sandboxes: In February 2017, the Autoriti Monetari Brunei Darussalam, the central bank, issued the FinTech Regulatory Sandbox Guidelines. It aims to aid development of fintech companies in the country through regulatory sandboxes.[b] In May 2018, Singapore and Brunei Darussalam signed the FinTech Cooperation Agreement to foster innovation in financial services between the two countries to facilitate information sharing and promote joint innovation projects. It established a framework for authorities to help fintech companies better understand the regulatory regime and opportunities in each jurisdiction.

[a] O. Clarke. 2018. The treatment of e-Money and virtual currencies across jurisdictions: A comparative table. https://www.osborneclarke.com/wp-content/uploads/2018/06/The-treatment-of-e-Money-and-virtual-currencies-across-jurisdictions.pdf.

[b] Bank Islam Brunei Darussalam. Guidelines No.Ftu/G-1/2017/1fintech Regulatory Sandbox Guidelines https://www.ambd.gov.bn/SiteAssets/fintech-office/FTSG%20v1_final.pdf.

Cambodia

Licensing e-money: E-money is regulated under Prakas No. B14-107-161 on the Management of Payment Service Provider.[a] Allows both banks and nonbanks to obtain licenses for providing payment services, including e-money issuance.

Digital banking: No digital banking license has been issued.

Open banking: No support to open banking implemented.

Peer-to-peer and marketplace lending: P2P lending is governed by the Law on Banking and Financial Institutions, primarily under the supervision of the National Bank of Cambodia and, to some extent, the Securities and Exchange Commission of Cambodia (SECC) if securities is the subject of the transaction.[b]

Equity crowdfunding: There does not appear to be any equity crowdfunding. The Law on the Issuance and Trading of Non-Government Securities is the primary legislation governing operation of the security market. The law stipulates conditions for both the issuing entity and platform. For a platform, approval from the director general of the SECC is required in accordance with article 23 of the law. The SECC will study and evaluate the issuance of related licenses based on its criteria set out in related decrees. For issuing entities, the Law on Securities sets out basic criteria to be able to issue securities.

Cryptoassets: Bank of Cambodia digital currency, which is a central bank digital currency, called Bakong, was launched on a trial basis in July 2019. The government had an agreement with 11 national banks to launch the digital currency.

Open APIs: No regulations.

Distributed ledger technology: One of the first countries to use blockchain technology in its national payments systems for use by consumers and commercial banks. Implemented during the second half of 2019 as an experiment to support financial inclusion and greater banking system efficiency. The application, known as the Bakong Project, connects financial institutions and payment providers and enables users to pay and make transactions in real time without fees.

Electronic know your customer (e-KYC): No regulations.

Cloud computing: No regulations.

Artificial intelligence: No regulations.

National digital ID enabling financial services: The coverage of national ID is around 89% of adults, however, access to the identity system by the financial sector is still being coordinated.

Data sharing, privacy, and protection: Cambodia's Ministry of Post and Telecommunications (MPTC) announced on 19 February 2021 that they will prepare a draft personal data protection law after finalizing their draft Cybercrime law. In addition, the recently enacted E-Commerce Law does contain data protection for all digital client data.

[a] Rajah & Tann Asia. 2017. NBC: New Provisions on Management of Payment Service Provider. Details of the National Bank of Cambodia's Prakas No. B14-107-161 on the Management of Payment Service Provider. https://kh.rajahtannasia.com/.

[b] Cambridge Center for Alternative Finance, Asian Development Bank Institute, FinTechSpace. 2019. The ASEAN Fintech Ecosystem Benchmarking Study. https://www.jbs.cam.ac.uk/wp-content/uploads/2020/08/2019-ccaf-asean-fintech-ecosystem-benchmarking-study.pdf.

[c] OneTrust DataGuidance Regulatory Research Software. Cambodia – Data Protection Overview September 2021 s://www.dataguidance.com/notes/cambodia-data-protection-overview

Indonesia

Licensing e-money: E-money regulation and supervision was initiated in 2009 under Bank Indonesia Regulation No: 11/12/PBI/2009. The regulation was recently amended in 2018 under Regulation No.20/6/PBI/2018. E-money transactions reached $1.1 billion in January 2020 (up 173% year over year) with e-money platforms growing to 41 as of February 2020.[a]

Digital banking: Digital banking regulation is governed by Financial Services Authority (OJK) Regulation No.12/POJK.03/2018 on the Implementation of Digital Services by Commercial Banks. The regulation allows commercial banks to seek OJK approval for providing electronic banking services. Banks must implement an electronic banking service plan for a maximum of 6 months after approval.[b]

Open banking: Bank Indonesia is urging the banking industry to develop open banking in the payment system through the formulation of Open Application Programming Interface (API) Standards, with links between the banking industry and financial technology. Open API standards are part of the Indonesia Payment System Blueprint for 2025.[c]

Peer-to-peer and marketplace lending: At the end of 2016, OJK issued OJK Regulation No. 77/POJK.01/2016 on Information Technology-Based Lending Services. The regulation is directed to support the growth of fintech P2P lending platforms. P2P platforms are classified as other financial services institutions. As of December 2019, 164 P2P companies were registered with OJK and 605,935 P2P lender accounts.[d]

Equity crowdfunding: OJK Rule No. 37/POJK.04/2018 on Equity Crowdfunding sets out regulations for equity crowdfunding. It is aimed at boosting economic growth in Indonesia by providing access to start-up companies and SMEs in raising funds electronically for development of their businesses.[e]

Cryptoassets: Indonesia's Commodity Futures Trading Regulatory Agency (known as Bappebti), part of the Ministry of Trade, issued four regulations in February 2019 that provide a legal framework for "the trading of crypto assets as commodities that could become the subjects of futures contracts and other derivative contracts traded in the stock market."[f] Indonesia continues to see exponential growth in crypto asset trading. The total value of crypto asset transactions was 64.7 trillion rupiah in 2020 but this has grown to over Rp370.4 trillion in the first 5 months of 2021. It is clear that Indonesia only allows crypto assets for investments, not payment purposes.

Open APIs: Bank Indonesia is urging the banking industry to develop open banking in the payment system through formulation of Open API Standards with interlinkages between the banking industry and financial technology (FinTech). Open API standards are part of the Indonesia Payment System Blueprint for 2025.

Distributed ledger technology: In its regulation for cryptoassets, Regulation No. 5/2019 defines a "Crypto Asset" as "an intangible commodity in the form of a digital asset that uses cryptography, a peer-to-peer network and distributed ledger technology to regulate the creation of new units, verify transactions and ensure transaction security without the involvement of a third party intermediary.

Electronic know-your-customer (e-KYC): In line with the Indonesia Payment Systems Blueprint 2025, e-KYC or digital KYC is seen as an important tool for balancing innovation, consumer protection, integrity, stability, and fair competition.

Cloud computing: The use of cloud services is considered to be an "outsourcing arrangement" and subject to regulatory supervision by the OJK.[g]

Financial Service Institutions must report on any intended outsourcing arrangements to the OJK and obtain approval. Cloud services would be considered outsourcing arrangements subject to this approval requirement.

Artificial intelligence: OJK issued a comprehensive regulation on fintech on August 18, 2018. The regulation deals with artificial intelligence/machine learning, machine readable news, social sentiment, big data, market information platforms, and automated data collection and analysis.

National digital ID enabling financial services: Thirteen financial institutions, including mobile payment service providers and P2P lending platforms, have been granted access to the government's civil registry data to expedite data verification and to prevent fraud and accelerate financial inclusion. These include the national ID system (e-KTP), which covers 86% of the Indonesian population.[h]

Data sharing, privacy, and protection: Indonesia has a diverse institutional infrastructure for data sharing focused on the small and medium-sized enterprise (SME) segment, including a credit bureau, a rating agency for SMEs, and credit guarantee and re-guarantee companies for SMEs.[i]

Innovation hubs, accelerators, and regulatory sandboxes: OJK and Bank Indonesia each provide mechanisms to test and pilot fintech initiatives to facilitate innovation. OJK has designed a procedure to allow fintech companies to deploy operations for a year after registration. During this time, OJK may conduct continuous evaluation of their performance. Within 1 year of registration, at most, companies must apply for a license (OJK 2017). Bank Indonesia enacted rules in December 2017 for the creation of a regulatory sandbox designed to support innovation while preserving customer protection and stability. Providers under this scheme would be able to start commercial operations within a defined period.[g]

---

[a] *The Jakarta Post*. 2020. E-Money Transactions in Indonesia Skyrocket. 27 February. https://www.thejakartapost.com/news/2020/02/27/e-money-transactions-in-indonesia-skyrocket-173-in-january.html.

[b] Deloitte. 2018. New Financial Services Authority (OJK) & Banking Regulations. KM No.5. https://www2.deloitte.com/content/dam/Deloitte/id/Documents/audit/id-aud-ojk-banking-regulations-aug2018.pdf.

[c] Bank Indonesia. 2020. Open API Standards and Bank Interlinkages with FinTechs for Payment Service Providers. Consultative Paper. Jakarta.

[d] S. Yuniarni and D. Chuo. 2020. Higher Returns Lead to P2P Boom in Indonesia. *Nikkei Asian Review*. 11 March. https://asia.nikkei.com/Business/Startups/Higher-returns-lead-to-P2P-boom-in-Indonesia.

[e] S. Batunanggar. 2019. Fintech Development and Regulatory Frameworks in Indonesia. *ADBI Working Paper Series*. Tokyo.

[f] Library of Congress. Regulatory Approaches to Crypto Assets: Indonesia. Database. (Accessed November 2020). https://www.loc.gov/law/help/crypto assets/indonesia.php. See also Forkast. 2021. *Indonesia Regulators Play Catch-up as Crypto Investment Soars*. July 23, https://forkast.news/indonesian-regulators-crypto-investment-soars/

[g] Asia Cloud Computing Association. 2015. *Asia's Financial Services: Ready for the Cloud: A Report on FSI Regulations Impacting Cloud in Asia Pacific Markets*. https://www.syciplaw.com/Documents/LegalResources/ACCA_Report_-_Web.pdf.

[h] Y. Prasidya. 2020. Thirteen Financial Institutions Get Access to Government's Civil Registry Database. *The Jakarta Post*. 12 June.

[i] World Bank and Association of Southeast Asian Nations. 2019. Advancing Digital Financial Inclusion in ASEAN.

Lao People's Democratic Republic

Licensing e-money: No regulation.

Digital banking: No digital banking license has been issued.

Open banking: No support to open banking implemented.

Peer-to-peer and marketplace lending: No record on the number of P2P lending participants or the volume of transactions in the country.

Equity crowdfunding: Equity crowdfunding is inactive. No records exist of crowdfunding platform operators or foreign crowdfunding platforms approved to operate. The laws and regulations require that securities be issued by public companies and offered in the capital market in accordance with the approval of the Bank of Laos.[a]

Cryptoassets: People are unfamiliar with the technology and Bank of Laos has issued a notice warning against the risks of cryptocurrencies.[b] Under the Law on Payment System, payment instruments do not include cryptocurrencies.

Open APIs: No regulation.

Distributed ledger technology: No regulation.

Electronic know-your-customer (e-KYC): No regulation.

Cloud computing: No regulation.

Artificial intelligence: No regulation.

National digital ID enabling financial services: The coverage of national ID is around 41% of adults and the country is currently piloting digitized foundational ID systems.

Data sharing, privacy, and protection: No announced plans to introduce comprehensive data sharing, privacy, and protection frameworks.

Innovation hubs, accelerators, and regulatory sandboxes: No regulation.

---

[a] World Trade Organization. 2019. Trade Policy Review: Lao People's Democratic Republic. Report by the Secretariat. https://www.wto.org/english/tratop_e/tpr_e/s394_e.pdf.

[b] J. Yap. 2018. Bank of Laos Warns Public against Use of Cryptocurrencies. *Laotian Times*. 31 August. https://laotiantimes.com/2018/08/31/bank-laos-warns-cryptocurrencies/.

Malaysia

Licensing e-money: Bank Negara Malaysia (BNM) has issued more than 50 e-money licenses and has witnessed substantial growth in e-payments, with increased competition and growing consumer adoption.[a] E-money is seen as a sharia-compliant payment instrument.[b]

Digital banking: BNM is finalizing its digital bank policy document and will open the application process in mid-2020. Up to five licenses are expected to be issued in 2020.

Open banking: Malaysia has established a nonmandatory framework for open banking. BNM also set up an open API implementation group in 2018, focused on developing standards on open data, security, access rights, and oversight arrangements for third-party payment providers, and to review existing customer information regulations.

Peer-to-peer and marketplace lending: P2P lending is governed by the Capital Markets and Services Act, 2007 and regulated by the Securities Commission Malaysia (SCM). On 13 April 2016, the SCM issued the Guidelines on Recognized Markets to regulate the practice of P2P. Where an Islamic investment note is executed on a P2P platform, the operator must ensure the trust account is sharia-compliant.

Equity crowdfunding: Supervised by the SCM. In April 2020, the SCM lifted fundraising limits on equity crowdfunding platforms, and allowed them and P2P financing schemes to operationalize secondary trading with immediate effect because of micro, small, and medium-sized enterprises interest to tap alternative fundraising channels to expand access to alternative capital and financing for small and medium-sized enterprises.

Cryptoassets: The SCM started regulating cryptocurrency exchanges in January 2019 under the Capital Markets and Services Digital Currency and Digital Token Order.[c]

Open APIs: The BNM invited qualified fintech providers to tender APIs under their open API platform in March 2020.[d]

Distributed ledger technology (DLT): The SCM and BNM have several initiatives underway directed at the use of DLT to facilitate financial services.[e]

Electronic know-your-customer (e-KYC): BNM issued an exposure draft in December 2019 that sets out the proposed requirements and guidance in implementing e-KYC for the onboarding of individuals to the finance sector.[f]

Cloud computing: Financial institutions using cloud computing must follow the new policy guidance on risk management in technology.[g]

Artificial intelligence: Guidance on artificial intelligence and machine learning algorithms is covered under the e-KYC exposure draft.[h]

National digital ID enabling financial services: The Digital Identity Verification Platform is for government and private service sector use, mainly to meet the need to verify the identity of individuals who have accessed electronic services, perform transactions, and provide digital signatures.[i]

Data sharing, privacy, and protection: BNM issued guidance to the finance sector under its "Management of Customer Information and Permitted Disclosures."[j]

Innovation hubs, accelerators, and regulatory sandboxes: BNM's regulatory sandbox serves as a platform to enable innovative solutions to be deployed and tested in a live environment, but within specified parameters and time frames.[k]

[a] R. Yunus. 2019. E-Money Hits Near RM40b in 5 Years. The Malaysian Reserve. 27 August. https://themalaysianreserve.com/2019/08/27/e-money-hits-near-rm40b-in-5-years; Cultivate Trends. 2020. *Key Developments in Mobile eWallets Payments in Malaysia.* https://cultivatetrends.com/key-developments-in-mobile-ewallets-payments-in-malaysia/.

[b] Sharia Advisory Council. 2020. The Sharia Advisory Council of Bank Negara Malaysia Ruling on E-Money as a Sharia Compliant Instrument. 201st SAC Meeting. 29–30 January. https://www.bnm.gov.my/documents/SAC/03_SAC201_Statement_eMoney_en.pdf.

[c] SCM. Digital Assets. https://www.sc.com.my/development/digital/digitalassets.

[d] BNM. Procurement Notices: Open Application Programing Interface Platform. https://www.bnm.gov.my/index.php?ch=en_tender&pg=en_tender_rfp&ac=5845&lang=en.

[e] MyGovernment. 2019. Blockchain and Distributed Ledger Technology (DLT) Initiatives in Malaysia 2019. https://www.malaysia.gov.my/portal/content/30633.

[f] BNM. 2019. Exposure Draft on Electronic Know You Customer (e-KYC). https://www.bnm.gov.my/index.php?ch=57&pg=543&ac=867&bb=file.

[g] BNM. 2020. Risk Management in Technology (RMiT). https://www.bnm.gov.my/ index.php?ch=57&pg=543&ac=816&bb=file.

[h] MAS. n.d. Principles to Promote Fairness, Ethics, Accountability and Transparency (FEAT) in the Use of Artificial Intelligence and Data Analytics in Singapore's Financial Sector. https://www.mas.gov.sg/~/media/MAS/News%20and%20Publications/Monographs%20and%20Information%20Papers/FEAT%20Principles%20Final.pdf.

[i] My Government. National Digital Identity Initiative. https://www.malaysia.gov.my/portal/ content/30592.

[j] BNM. 2017. Management of Customer Information and Permitted Disclosures. https://www.bnm.gov.my/index.php?ch=57&pg=144&ac=632&bb=file.

[k] BNM. 2020. Annual Report 2019. Unlocking the Potential of Innovation: Preparing for a Digital Future. Kuala Lumpur. https://www.bnm.gov.my/ar2019/files/ar2019_en_box3.pdf.

Philippines

Licensing e-money: Bangko Sentral ng Pilipinas (BSP) in 2004 became one of the first in the region to allow e-money services by nonbanks. It licensed e-money formally in September 2009 under circular 649.[a]

Digital banking: BSP granted the first two virtual bank licenses in 2019 and more are licenses are being reviewed.

Open banking: BSP issued circular no 1122 on 10 June 2021 that covers a consent-driven Open Finance Framework focused on portability, interoperability, and collaboration among financial institutions and third-party providers.

Peer-to-peer and marketplace lending: P2P platforms must register with the Securities and Exchange Commission (SEC). While the BSP does not directly regulate P2P lenders, the Truth and Lending Act does apply to all lenders and the Data Privacy Act is being utilized to protect fintech lending consumers.

Equity crowdfunding: In 2019, the SEC issued rules and regulations on crowdfunding with a focus on small and medium-sized enterprise finance.[b]

Cryptoassets: Crypto assets were legalized and crypto asset exchanges were regulated by the BSP under Circular 944. However, Circular No. 1108 issued on 21 January 2021 revised the definition of crypto assets and exchanges to virtual assets and virtual exchanges in light of the new FATF guidelines that were to be issued in 2021.[c]

Open APIs: Under the Open Finance Framework, the BSP is consulting with the newly formed Open Finance Oversight Committee to develop and agree upon open API standards.

Distributed ledger technology (DLT): The BSP is working closely with market innovators and industry players to explore tie-ups of correspondent banks with DLT providers. These initiatives are still being monitored under the BSP's regulatory sandbox.[d]

Electronic know-your-customer (e-KYC): Even though the Philippines is still working on the implementation of a national ID system, the BSP has been developing various e-KYC approaches to onboard new customers.[e]

Cloud computing: Cloud computing is allowed by the BSP under the Enhanced Guidelines on Information Security Management. With support from the Asian Development Bank, the BSP has also experimented with and used cloud computing to expand financial inclusion in the Philippines.[f]

Artificial intelligence: The BSP has not issued any guidance on this topic.

National digital ID enabling financial services: As part of its financial inclusion initiatives, the BSP has reached a government-to-government deal with the Philippine Statistics Authority to provide the country's biometric national identification card. Implementation is ongoing.[g]

Data sharing, privacy, and protection: Data sharing, privacy, and protection are governed by the Data Privacy Act and implemented by the Data Privacy Commission.[h] The commission handled violations by 48 fintech lenders in 2019.

Innovation hubs, accelerators, and regulatory sandboxes: The BSP was one of the earliest innovators, launching one of the first regulatory sandboxes, called the "test-and-learn approach" in 2004, which allowed the central bank to permit e-money issuers under a letter of no-objection. Since then, the BSP has strengthened its fintech initiatives by launching a dedicated financial technology subsector unit as well the Technology Risk and Innovation Supervision Department, which is primarily responsible for conducting on-site and offsite IT supervision of regulated entities. It is maintaining a comprehensive and flexible regulatory framework relating to IT supervision. The Technology Risk and Innovation Supervision Department is in charge of cybersecurity surveillance and promoting digital or fintech innovation through the BSP's regulatory sandbox.[i]

[a] BSP. 2009. BSP Circular 649. http://www.bsp.gov.ph/downloads/Regulations/attachments/2009/c649.pdf.

[b] Securities and Exchange Commission. 2019. SEC Approves Rules on Crowdfunding. Press release. https://www.sec.gov.ph/pr-2019/sec-approves-rules-on-crowdfunding/.

[c] BSP. 2017. http://www.bsp.gov.ph/downloads/regulations/attachments/2017/c944.pdf.

[d] BSP. 2018. Providing an Enabling Environment at the Crossroads of Digital Transformation. Speech delivered at the Annual Convention of the Association of Philippine Correspondent Bank Officers. Puerto Princesa. 30 June. http://www.bsp.gov.ph/publications/speeches.asp?id=616.

[e] ePay Pilipinas. 2017. BSP Crafts Rules for Electronic KYC Procedures. http://www.epaypilipinas.com/bsp-crafts-rules-electronic-kyc-procedures/.

[f] M. Valenzuela and J. Izaguirre. 2019. Cloud Computing for Financial Inclusion: Lessons from the Philippines. *CGAP Blog*. 24 September. https://www.cgap.org/blog/cloud-computing-financial-inclusion-lessons-philippines.

[g] BSP. 2019. Financial Inclusion Initiatives. http://www.bsp.gov.ph/downloads/Publications /2019/microfinance_2019.pdf.

[h] National Privacy Commission. 2012. Republic Act 10173—Data Privacy Act of 2012. https://www.privacy.gov.ph/data-privacy-act/.

[i] B. Diokno. 2019. Inclusion and Digital Transformation—A Collaborative Approach to Regulating Fintech. Speech delivered at the Finance Executives Breakfast Roundtable. Manila. 11 October. https://www.bis.org/review/r191023g.htm.

Singapore

Licensing e-money: Expanded e-money licensing under the Payment Services Act has increased the number of nonbank fintech e-money providers, increased competition, and lowered costs, boosting customer usage.[a]

Digital banking: The Monetary Authority of Singapore (MAS) launched new digital bank license offerings in 2019 and received 21 applications by 31 December 2019.

Open banking: To support open banking, MAS published an application programming interface (API) playbook in 2018. To date, Singapore's API Register has logged 121 transactional and 192 informational APIs.[b]

Peer-to-peer and marketplace lending: Singapore has no direct regulations on P2P lending, but its principles of promoting fairness, ethics, accountability, and transparency govern all lenders, including P2P platforms.

Equity crowdfunding: MAS administers equity-based crowdfunding the same way it governs debt-based crowdfunding. For both cases, the crowdfunding platform must have a capital markets service license. If a platform also offers financial advice on investment, it should hold a license to act as a financial advisor; see Financial Advisers Act (Cap. 110).

Cryptoassets: MAS previously took an open approach to cryptocurrency exchanges, but the new Payment Services Act now provides for stricter anti-money-laundering (AML) and combating the financing of terrorism (CFT) regulations.[c]

Open APIs: The MAS Financial Industry API Register serves as the initial landing site for open APIs available in the financial industry. It is updated on an ongoing basis as Singapore's financial institutions make their open APIs available.[d]

Distributed ledger technology (DLT): MAS has several initiatives in place to explore the use of DLT and blockchain to facilitate financial services, including cross-border financial transactions.[e]

Electronic know-your-customer (e-KYC): MAS is working with the Smart National Digital Government Office and the Government Technology Agency to develop the National Digital Identity platform, which will provide residents with a national means to prove their identity and sign documents digitally so they can transact conveniently and securely online.[f]

Cloud computing: Cloud computing is seen as a form of outsourcing and is encouraged by MAS.[g]

Artificial intelligence: MAS' Principles to Promote Fairness, Ethics, Accountability and Transparency in the Use of Artificial Intelligence and Data Analytics is seen as one of the most extensive guidelines in the region.[h]

National digital ID enabling financial services: Working with the Smart National Digital Government Office and the Government Technology Agency to develop the National Digital Identity Platform.

Data sharing, privacy, and protection: MAS-issued regulatory instruments relevant to data protection include the Notices and Guidelines on Technology Risk Management, MAS Notices and Guidelines on Prevention of Money Laundering and Countering the Financing of Terrorism, and the MAS Guidelines on Outsourcing. Broadly, these make clear that financial institutions may continue collecting, using, and disclosing personal data without customer consent for meeting AML and CFT requirements, and acknowledge customers' rights under the Personal Data Protection Act, 2012 to access and correct personal data in the possession or under the control of the financial institutions.[i]

Innovation hubs, accelerators, and regulatory sandboxes: MAS operates an innovation hub and an active regulatory sandbox.[j]

[a] Deloitte. 2019. Understanding the Regulatory Requirements of the MAS Payment Services Act. https://www2.deloitte.com/content/dam/Deloitte/sg/Documents/financial-services/sg-fsi-payment-services-act-2019-wns.pdf.

[b] Monetary Authority of Singapore. n.d. Application Programing Interfaces (APIs). https://www.mas.gov.sg/development/fintech/technologies---apis.

[c] MAS. 2019. Proposed Regulatory Approach for Derivatives Contracts on Payment Tokens. Consultation Paper on Proposed Regulatory Approach for Derivatives Contracts on Payment Tokens. https://www.crowdfundinsider.com/wp-content/uploads/2020/05/MAS-Consultation-Paper-on-Proposed-Regulatory-Approach-for-Derivatives-Contracts-on-Payment-Tokens-November-2019.pdf.

[d] MAS. Financial Industry API Register. https://www.mas.gov.sg/development/fintech/financial-industry-api-register.

[e] MAS. Blockchain/Distributed Ledger Technology. https://www.mas.gov.sg/development/ fintech/technologies---blockchain-and-dlt.

[f] MAS. Digital ID and e-KYC. https://www.mas.gov.sg/development/fintech/technologies---digital-id-and-e-kyc.

[g] MAS. Cloud. https://www.mas.gov.sg/development/fintech/technologies---cloud.

[h] MAS. Principles to Promote Fairness, Ethics, Accountability and Transparency (FEAT) in the Use of Artificial Intelligence and Data Analytics in Singapore's Financial Sector. https://www.mas.gov.sg/~/media/MAS/News%20and%20Publications/Monographs%20and%20Information%20Papers/FEAT%20Principles%20Final.pdf.

[i] MAS. Guidelines to Mas Notice PS-N02 on Prevention of Money Laundering and Countering the Financing of Terrorism. https://www.mas.gov.sg/-/media/MAS/Regulations-and-Financial-Stability/Regulatory-and-Supervisory-Framework/Anti_Money-Laundering_Countering-the-Financing-of-Terrorism/Guidelines-to-PSN02-on-Prevention-of-Money-Laundering-and-Countering-the-Financing-of-Terrorism--DPT.pdf

[j] MAS. Overview of Regulatory Sandbox. https://www.mas.gov.sg/development/fintech/regulatory-sandbox.

Thailand

Licensing e-money: The Bank of Thailand (BOT) issues permits for nonfinancial institutions that issue e-money. E-money issuers are covered under B.E. Notification of the Ministry of Finance: Businesses that Require a Permit under Section 5 of the Notification of the Revolution Council No. 58 (Business of Electronic Money Card) dated 4 October 2004.[a] E-money is also covered under the Payment System Act B.E. 2560 (2017).[b]

Digital banking: The BOT is extending the scope of business of commercial banks to include IT-related services to support digital banking.[c]

Open banking: While there is no regulation on open banking in Thailand, several banks have developed open APIs and are partnering with third-parties to offer open banking services.[d]

Peer-to-peer and marketplace lending: On 29 April 2019, the BOT issued Notification 4/2562. The notification is the first legislation relating to P2P lending, and provides a number of parameters within which P2P platform providers and lenders must operate.[e]

Equity crowdfunding: The Electronic System or Network (ECF) regulatory framework has been set out by the Capital Markets Supervisory Board, predominantly in two regulations that have been in effect since 16 May 2015: (i) Notification of the Capital Market Supervisory Board (No. TorJor. 7/2558, Re: Regulations on Offer for Sale of Securities through Electronic System or Network (ECF Notification); and (ii) Notification of the Securities and Exchange Commission (No. KorJor. 3/2558 Re: Exemption from Filing of Registration Statement for Securities Offered through Provider of Electronic System or Network) (Exemption Notification).[f]

Cryptoassets: The Royal Decree on the Digital Asset Businesses, B.E. 2561, regulates the crypto sector. It categorizes digital asset businesses as "digital asset exchange," "digital asset broker," and "digital asset dealer."[g] The BOT, with a number of banks, was developing a wholesale central bank digital currency to facilitate interbank settlements and cross-border payments.[h]

Open APIs: Open banking services are growing rapidly in Thailand, with at least three banks partnering with fintech providers to offer open banking services. In January 2018, the Securities and exchange Commission launched its API developer portal for financial product information, exchange rates, and more.[j]

Distributed ledger technology (DLT): The BOT launched Project Inthanon in 2018 to explore and experiment in the application of DLT in the financial system.[k]

Electronic know-your-customer (e-KYC): The BOT has introduced a new regulation to facilitate KYC by using an electronic means (e-KYC) for account opening, deposit acceptance, or fund acceptance from public. BOT Notification No. SorNorSor. 7/2559 Re: Criteria in Taking Deposits or Taking Money from the Public.[l]

Cloud computing: The BOT has permitted financial institutions to outsource IT activities to service providers, in the country or abroad. Institutions that seek to use cloud computing must get prior approval from the BOT.[m]

Artificial intelligence: In 2019, the Digital Economy and Society Ministry drafted the artificial intelligence ethics guidelines. The draft is not yet final or enforced.[n]

National digital ID enabling financial services: The Electronic Transactions Development Agency is working on legislation to replace physical ID cards with the Digi-ID. Government, banks, and insurance companies have been using digital identities since 2018. Thailand has a National Digital Identity Platform which allows a user's data to be securely exchanged, complete with blockchain and facial recognition verification requirements.[o]

Data sharing, privacy, and protection: In May 2019, the Personal Data Protection Act became law. Under the law, individuals have the right to control how their personal data is collected, stored, disseminated, and protected to protect their privacy and manage personal data collected by organizations and companies. This law came into full effect on June 1, 2021.[p]

Innovation hubs, accelerators, and regulatory sandboxes: The BOT launched a regulatory sandbox in December 2016 to accommodate provision of financial services which leverage new technologies.[q] In March 2017, the Office of Insurance Commission announced its intention to launch an "InsurTech" sandbox, allowing agents, insurers, and fintech to test innovative products. SEC Thailand also launched a series of regulatory sandboxes for securities, derivatives, clearing houses, KYC, and e-trading.

[a] Bank of Thailand (BOT). Related Laws & Regulations. https://www.bot.or.th/English/PaymentSystems/OversightOfEmoney/RelatedLaw/Pages/default.aspx.

[b] BOT. Payment Systems Act B.E. 2560 (2017). https://www.bot.or.th/English/PaymentSystems/PSA_Oversight/Pages/default.aspx#:~:text=2560%20(2017)&text=Those%20intending%20to%20undertake%20the,be%2C%20prior%20to%20business%20commencement.

[c] Notification of the Bank of ThailandNo.FPG.18/2562.

[d] Fintech Singapore News. 2021. The State of Open Banking in Thailand in 2021. 5 March https://fintechnews.sg/49397/openbanking/the-state-open-banking-in-thailand/

[e] *Conventus Law.* 2019. First Peer-To-Peer Lending Regulation Issued by the Bank of Thailand. 7 June. http://www.conventuslaw.com/report/first-peer-to-peer-lending-regulation-issued-by/.

[f] Association of Southeast Asian Nations (ASEAN). 2017. Facilitation Equity Crowdfunding in the ASEAN Region. https://asean.org/wp-content/uploads/2017/09/Final-Facilitating-Equity-Crowdfunding-in-ASEAN.pdf.

[g] K. Helms. 2020. Thailand Has Now Licensed 13 Cryptocurrency Service Providers. *Bitcoin.com.* 4 November. https://news.bitcoin.com/thailand-licensed-13-cryptocurrency-service-providers/.

[h] BOT. 2020. The Bank of Thailand Announces the Prototype Development Project of Central Bank Digital Currency (CBDC). Press Release No. 30/2020. https://www.bot.or.th/English/PressandSpeeches/Press/2020/Pages/n3063.aspx.

[i] Finextra. 2019. The Asia-Pacific Way of Open Banking Regulation. 20 June. https://www.finextra.com/blogposting/17396/the-asia-pacific-way-of-open-banking-regulation.

[j] G. Rothwell. 2018. The brave new world of Open Banking in APAC: Thailand. *Accenture.* 28 November.

[k] BOT. Inthanon. Phase 1. https://www.bot.or.th/Thai/PaymentSystems/Documents/Inthanon_Phase1_Report.pdf.

[l] K. Kietduriyakul. 2016. Electronic Know-Your-Customer (e-KYC): Anti-Money Laundering in Thailand in the Digital Era. *Global Compliance News.* 15 September. https://globalcompliancenews.com/electronic-know-your-customer-e-kyc-anti-money-laundering-in-digital-era-20160915/.

[m] BOT. Notification of the Bank of ThailandNo. FPG. 19/2559Re: Regulations on IT Outsourcing for Business Operations of Financial Institutions.

[n] *OpenGov Asia.* 2019. Thailand Drafts Ethics Guidelines for AI. 4 November. https://opengovasia.com/thailand-drafts-ethics-guidelines-for-ai/.

[o] S. Rigby. 2020. What's Next for Thailand's Covid-19. 19 August. recovery?https://govinsider.asia/transformation/whats-next-for-thailands-covid-19-recovery/.

[p] *DLA Piper.* Data Protection Laws of the World. Thailand. https://www.dlapiperdataprotection.com/index.html?t=law&c=TH&c2=.

[q] BOT. List of Peer-to-Peer Lending Platform Providers Participating in the BOT Regulatory Sandbox. https://www.bot.or.th/English/PaymentSystems/FinTech/Pages/P2PLendingSandbox.aspx.

Viet Nam

Licensing e-money: The State Bank of Vietnam recognizes e-money as a financial settlement service and authorizes licenses to a number of mobile payment companies. As of the end of August 2019, only 31 companies were granted these licenses.

Digital banking: No regulation.

Open banking: No regulation.

Peer-to-peer and marketplace lending: The government will soon decide whether to allow pilot implementation of peer-to-peer (P2P) lending before officially developing laws for the new form of business.[a]

Equity crowdfunding: Vietnam's State Bank and the Ministry of Finance are studying options to introduce equity crowdfunding.

Cryptoassets: The government does not authorize use of the cryptoassets, because it does not constitute a legitimate means of payment under the currency and banking legal regulations (96/2014/ND-CP).

Open APIs: The State Bank of Vietnam has been working on a draft circular for the application of open API in the banking sector. The central bank has been partnering with Japan's NTT Data Company to test-run an Open API open canvas solution.[b]

Distributed ledger technology (DLT): Government is planning to enact laws for DLT, and until the law is enacted, it is expected that DLT business will not be legally protected.

Electronic know-your-customer (e-KYC): In a recent regulatory development, transactions involving high technologies no longer need to involve in-person meetings when establishing customer relationships for the first time. Instead, anti-money laundering reporting entities could take the initiative to apply alternative measures.[c]

Cloud computing: The Ministry of Information and Communications has issued technical criteria and specifications for cloud computing solutions for e-government deployment.

Artificial intelligence: In December 2019, the central bank set the goal that, by 2025, a regulatory framework will be issued for the application of key 4.0 technologies, including those for KYC, open API, Big Data, artificial intelligence, blockchain, and cloud computing.[d]

National digital ID enabling financial services: The Ministry of Information and Communications announced the launch of akaChain, an enterprise blockchain platform developed by FPT Software, as part of its national program for digital transformation, including the development of digital ID solutions.[e]

Data sharing, privacy, and protection: On 1 January 2019, the Cyber Security Act was implemented. Under it, all services operating must strictly comply with the country's unique regulations.

Innovation hubs, accelerators, and regulatory sandboxes: The government issued Resolution 01 in January 2020 outlining the regulatory sandbox for fintech banking and cashless payments.

[a] *Vietnam News.* 2019. Government Moves to Legalise P2P Lending. 13 March.

[b] L. Chi Dang. n.d. Vietnam: Fintech Regulatory Landscape in Vietnam. Baker McKenzie. https://www.lexology.com/library/detail.aspx?g=0d0303af-6a2e-4301-b61d-8175e1f8e6c3.

[c] Baker & McKenzie *Global Compliance News.* 2020. 26 June. Vietnam: Fintech regulatory landacape in Vietnam. https://globalcompliancenews.com/vietnam-fintech-regulatory-landscape-in-vietnam-11062020/.

[d] McKinsey & Company. n.d. FinTechnicolor: The New Picture in Finance. Report. New York. https://www.mckinsey.com/~/media/mckinsey/industries/financial%20services/our%20insights/bracing%20for%20seven%20critical%20changes%20as%20fintech%20matures/fintechnicolor-the-new-picture-in-finance.ashx.

[e] *Business Wire.* 2020. Vietnam's Government Endorses FPY Software's Blockchain Platform, Pushing for National Digital Transformation. 17 August. https://www.businesswire.com/news/home/20200817005299/en/Vietnam's-Government-Endorses-FPT-Software's-Blockchain-Platform-Pushing-for-National-Digital-Transformation.

Source: Authors' compilation.

OTHER COUNTRIES

Australia

Licensing e-money: A range of stored-value facilities encompasses prepaid funds that can be used to make payments. The Council of Financial Regulators initiated a review of the regulatory framework for stored-value facilities in Australia in mid-2018. Recommendations on a revised regulatory framework are being developed.[a]

Digital banking: The Australian Prudential Regulation Authority (APRA) introduced the Restricted Authorised Deposit-Taking Institutions License, which provides eligible applicants a restricted license for a maximum of 2 years before they must meet the prudential framework in full to qualify for an ADI license. This new regulatory route is particularly suited to digital or neo banks.[b] At least four digital banks operate in Australia.

Open banking: Open banking under the Consumer Data Right Act allows Australian consumers to share banking data with third-party providers. The Australian Competition and Consumer Commission oversees the data sharing regime.[c]

Peer-to-peer and marketplace lending: Under financial services and credit laws, providers of marketplace lending products and related services will generally need to hold (i) an Australian financial services license and (ii) an Australian credit license if loans made through the platform are consumer loans (e.g., loans to individuals for domestic, personal, or household purposes).[d]

Equity crowdfunding: In March 2017, the Australian Parliament enacted the Corporations Amendment (Crowd-Sourced Funding) Act 2017 to introduce equity crowdfunding. The Australian Securities and Investments Commission is responsible for market conduct and consumer protection and oversight of securities regulation; as such, it is responsible for oversight of the Australian equity crowdfunding regulatory regime.[e]

Cryptoassets: Whether cryptoassets are a type of financial product under the Corporations Act 2001 depends on their nature, says the Australian Securities and Investments Commission. Where tokens created through blockchain are considered to be an interest in a managed investment scheme, shares, derivatives, or a non-cash payment facility, an entity that deals with or provides custodial services with respect to such tokens could be providing financial services, with disclosure and licensing requirements applying. If the tokens are not financial products, the Australian Consumer Law would apply.[f]

Open application programming interface (API): The Australian Treasury has developed an open banking framework that will require banks to join an API-based data-sharing platform with clear guidelines about data security and privacy controls as well as corresponding penalties for violation of the rules. Phase 1 took effect in July 2019.[g]

Distributed ledger technology: The Australian Securities and Investments Commission believes the existing regulatory framework is able to accommodate existing digital ledger technology (DLT) use. However, as DLT matures, it anticipates additional regulatory considerations.[h]

Electronic know-your-customer (e-KYC): Australian Transaction Reports and Analysis Centre provides KYC procedures for all reporting entities. Reliable and independent documentation or electronic data (or both) to verify information about the customer and beneficial owner must be used. The Document Verification Service managed by the Department of Home Affairs can verify data electronically.[i] The analysis center also released guidelines on compliance with requirements during the coronavirus disease (COVID-19) pandemic given the challenges posed by social distancing.[j]

Cloud computing: Regulated institutions must comply with the APRA Prudential Standard CPS 231 Outsourcing when outsourcing a material business activity. APRA published specific, detailed guidance in its information paper. Outsourcing involving cloud computing services to help regulated entities assess cloud providers and services more effectively and guide them through the regulatory issues of outsourcing to the cloud. When outsourcing, including to a cloud service, regulated institutions must also review and consider their ongoing compliance with APRA Prudential Standard CPS 234 Information Security.[k]

Artificial intelligence: The government released its Artificial Intelligence Technology Roadmap in November 2019 to accompany a standards and national ethics framework.[l]

National digital identification (ID) enabling financial services: The Digital Transformation Agency is responsible for developing a National Digital ID Platform.[m]

Data sharing, privacy, and protection: Australia regulates data privacy and protection through a mix of federal, state, and territory laws. The Federal Privacy Act 1988 and Australian Privacy Principles apply to private sector entities with an annual turnover of at least A$3 million, and all Commonwealth Government and Australian Capital Territory Government agencies. Most states and territories (except Western Australia and South Australia) have their own data protection legislation applicable to state government agencies and private businesses that interact with state government agencies.[n]

Innovation hubs, accelerators, and regulatory sandboxes: The government introduced the enhanced regulatory sandbox, which allows testing of services or activities without first obtaining a financial or credit services license. The Australian Securities and Investments Commission oversees the sandbox.[o]

[a] Reserve Bank of Australia. n.d. Payments System Board Annual Report – 2019. https://www.rba.gov.au/publications/annual-reports/psb/2019/retail-payments-regulation-and-policy-issues.html.

[b] M. Bracken et al. 2019. Australia: Digital Banks and Neo Banks - Restricted ADI Licence Regime. Mondaq.4 September.

[c] *Finextra*. 2020. Australia Takes First Steps Towards Open Banking. 1 July. https://www.finextra.com/newsarticle/36131/australia-takes-first-steps-towards-open-banking.

[d] Australian Securities and Investments Commission. n.d. Marketplace Lending (Peer-to-Peer Lending) Products. https://asic.gov.au/regulatory-resources/financial-services/marketplace-lending/marketplace-lending-peer-to-peer-lending-products/.

[e] The ASEAN Secretariat. 2017. Facilitating Equity Crowdfunding in the ASEAN Region. Jakarta. https://asean.org/wp-content/uploads/2017/09/Final-Facilitating-Equity-Crowdfunding-in-ASEAN.pdf.

[f] Library of Congress. n.d. Regulatory Approaches to Cryptoassets: Australia. https://www.loc.gov/law/help/cryptoassets/australia.php#:~:text=The%20Australian%20Securities%20and%20Investments,Cth)%20depends%20on%20their%20nature.&text=Both%20this%20law%20and%20the%20Corporations%20Act%20prohibit%20false%20and%20misleading%20conduct; https://asic.gov.au/regulatory-resources/digital-transformation/initial-coin-offerings-and-crypto-assets/.

[g] *Kapronasia*. 2019. How Will Open Banking Change Australia's Financial Sector? 10 October. https://www.kapronasia.com/research/blog/how-will-open-banking-change-australia-s-financial-sector.html.

[h] Australian Securities and Investments Commission. n.d. Evaluating Distributed Ledger Technology. https://asic.gov.au/regulatory-resources/digital-transformation/evaluating-distributed-ledger-technology/#framework.

[i] Australian Transaction Reports and Analysis Centre (AUSTRAC). n.d. Reliable and Independent Documentation and Electronic Data. Australian Government. https://www.austrac.gov.au/business/how-comply-and-report-guidance-and-resources/customer-identification-and-verification/reliable-and-independent-documentation-and-electronic-data.

[j] AUSTRAC. n.d. How to Comply with KYC Requirements during the COVID-19 Pandemic. Australian Government. https://www.austrac.gov.au/business/how-comply-and-report-guidance-and-resources/customer-identification-and-verification/kyc-requirements-covid-19.

[k] Microsoft. 2020. Australian Prudential Regulation Authority. Overview. https://docs.microsoft.com/en-us/microsoft-365/compliance/offering-apra-australia?view=o365-worldwide.

[l] CSIRO. Artificial Intelligence Roadmap. https://data61.csiro.au/en/Our-Research/Our-Work/AI-Roadmap.

[m] Digital Transformation Agency. N.d. Digital Identity. Australian Government. https://www.dta.gov.au/our-projects/digital-identity.

[n] *DLA Piper*. Data Protection Laws of the World. Australia. https://www.dlapiperdataprotection.com/index.html?t=law&c=AU&c2=.

[o] Australian Securities and Investments Commission. n.d. Enhanced Regulatory Sandbox. https://asic.gov.au/for-business/innovation-hub/enhanced-regulatory-sandbox/.

People's Republic of China

Licensing e-money: E-money is regulated by the People's Bank of China (PRC).

Digital banking: Since 2014, the China Banking Regulatory Commission has licensed four digital-only banks—WeBank (2014), which is backed by Tencent; MYbank (2015), an Alibaba offshoot; AiBank (2017), backed by Baidu; and XW Bank (2016). The commission's E-banking Rule and E-banking Guideline seem to have established a comprehensive mechanism to regulate and oversee e-banking. Capital liquidity rules: e-banks are subject to the same regulatory requirements as any existing banks; Minimum Tier 1 Capital Adequacy Ratio: 8.5%; and minimum paid-in capital: $285 million (RMB2 billion).

Open banking: While open banking is recognized as an integral part of fintech, it is still considered in its infancy, lacking as it does universal industry standards and unsolved data security measures. In late 2019, the National Internet Finance Association of China, after a symposium on commercial banks' open banking business, proposed in a report that as open banking develops, a regulatory framework should be established to guard against systemic risks, and efforts should be made to formulate industry standards. Tencent-backed online lender WeBank has teamed up with Tencent's cloud platform to launch a new fintech research lab, which will be based upon the "development concept" of open banking, and engage in "joint research and technological innovation in the areas of basic frameworks, financial applications and experiential innovation."

Peer-to-peer and marketplace lending: The China Banking and Insurance Regulatory Commission regulates under the Provisional Rules for the Management of Services Activities of Internet Lending Information Intermediaries and Working Scheme for the Conditional Filing of Internet Lending Information Intermediaries.

Equity crowdfunding: China Securities Regulatory Commission, the regulatory body, is guided by legislation including the Administrative Measures for Sales of Securities Investment Fund and the Administrative Measures for Supervision of Money Market Funds.

Cryptoassets: On 15 September, 2021 the People's Bank of China issued a Notice on the Further Preventing and Handling the Risk of Speculation in Virtual Asset Transactions. This enhanced notice made crypto assets an illegal financing activity and banned all virtual asset service providers both within China and overseas exchanges servicing Chinese domestic residents.[a]

Open application programming interface (API): In January 2020, the PRC's financial authorities announced their plan to launch new regulations and policies for the open banking sector and open APIs. Authorities will also strengthen regulation of client-end software provided by financial institutions and expand filing for mobile financial apps from trial areas to the whole of the country.

Distributed ledger technology: The Cybersecurity Administration of China, the regulator, is guided by the Administrative Rule on Blockchain Information Service.

Electronic know-your-customer (e-KYC): In November 2018, the Act on Prevention of Transfer of Criminal Proceeds was amended to introduce new methods of verifying customer identity. Such verification can be completed by internet alone; for instance, when opening bank accounts via the internet.

The People's Bank of China has promulgated the Measures on the Administration of Customer Identify Verification and the Identification and Transaction Document Requirements for Financial Institutions.[b]

Cloud computing: A guideline was jointly issued by the internet regulator, the Cyberspace Administration of China, along with the National Development and Reform Commission, Ministry of Industry and Information Technology, and the Ministry of Finance. The guideline aims to increase the safety of cloud computing services specifically for users of the Party, government bodies, and key information infrastructure operators. It requires cloud platforms that provide government-facing solutions to submit applications for cloud computing service safety assessment, beginning in September 2019.

Artificial intelligence: In 2017, the State Council of the PRC published the Artificial Intelligence Development Plan. Municipal and provincial governments across the country are establishing cross-sector partnerships with research institutions and tech companies to create local artificial intelligence (AI) innovation ecosystems and drive rapid research and development. The city of Hangzhou, in Zhejiang Province, has established an "AI Town," clustering together the tech company Alibaba, Zhejiang University, and local businesses to collaborate on AI development.

National digital ID enabling financial services: Backed by the Ministry of Public Security's Research Institute and other bodies, such as major Chinese banks, the country is issuing digital versions of the national ID card as an alternative to the physical cards in use. The government is working with Tencent's WeChat, marketed as Weixin on the mainland, to host the digital card, as it is the most popular messaging app.

Data sharing, privacy, and protection: The new Civil Code, which will officially come into force by 2021, stipulated the principles of privacy and protection of personal information, defines the concept of personal information, sets out the legal basis for processing personal information, regulates the obligations of personal information processors, natural persons' rights to their personal information, and duties of administrative organs. It enshrined the right to the protection of personal information and merged existing laws on consumer rights and cybersecurity to expand protection of personal and private data. The legislative authority issued the draft Data Security Law, which was planned to be finalized within 2020; regulatory requirements relating to data security eventually will be reflected in law. The draft includes 7 sections and 55 articles, covering data security and industrial development, data security regulatory system, data security protection obligations, and government data security and access.

Innovation hubs, accelerators, and regulatory sandboxes: The People's Bank of China supported the launch of fintech innovation regulatory trials in Beijing and explored the establishment of a fintech innovation supervision tool in line with national conditions and international standards. This would guide licensed financial institutions in the use of modern IT to empower finance to improve quality and efficiency for complying with laws and regulations, and protecting consumer rights and interests and to create a defensive, safe, inclusive, and open financial technology innovation and development environment. The first set of trial applications will involve areas including the Internet of Things, micro and small loans, smart banking, and mobile phone points-of-sale.

[a] Baker McKenzie, 2021, Global Compliance News *China: Briefing on the People's Bank of China notice on further preventing and handling the risk of speculation in virtual currency transactions.* Oct 11. https://www.globalcompliancenews.com/2021/10/11/china-briefing-on-the-pboc-notice-on-further-preventing-and-handling-the-risk-of-speculation-in-virutal-currency-transactions-29092021/

[b] ICLG.com. China: Anti-Money Laundering Laws and Regulations 2020. 14 May.

India

Licensing e-money: The Reserve Bank of India (RBI) regulates the payment system in the country. eMoney consists of prepaid instruments issued as "wallets" and cards and is regulated under the Payment Settlement Systems Act 2007. These instruments facilitate purchase of goods and services, such as financial services and remittances, against the value stored on the instruments. The prepaid payment instruments are classified as either closed system, semi-closed system, or open system. RBI introduced prepaid instruments in December 2019, which can be loaded/re-loaded only from a bank account or a credit card and can be issued based on essential minimum details sourced from the customer. Such prepaid instruments can be used only for purchase of goods and services and not for funds transfer.

Digital banking: Retail neo banks, which arrived recently, are focused on the needs of retail customers—savings, payments, lending, and wealth. Many new players, with deep pockets, are still attempting to enter this space and there would be cutthroat competition in this segment. SME neo banks cater to the needs of small and medium-sized enterprises. These have always been different to retail and corporate segments, but most banks have always treated SMEs as a part of them. The real needs of SME customers, like invoicing, collections, and credit have never been catered to by banks. The segment is large enough to allow for more than five valuable SME neo banks.[a]

Open banking: To facilitate open banking, RBI has issued guidelines for regulation of nonbank financial companies—account aggregators in 2016. The account aggregators under contract retrieve or collect financial information (18 types of financial information have been specified) pertaining to its customer—as may be specified by the bank from time to time—and consolidate, organize, and present such information to the customer or other financial information user as may be specified by the bank. This is provided that the financial information pertaining to the customer is not the property of the account aggregator and not to be used in any other manner. Specific customer consent is required for the purpose/s for which the information is used and the organizations with whom the information is shared. The Reserve Bank of India Information Technology Private Limited has framed the application programming interface based on technical specifications for all the participants of the AA-ecosystem and published the same on its website. Such specifications ensure that movement of data is secure, duly authorized, smooth, and seamless between the participants, and ensures that data privacy is maintained. Further, IndiaStack is a set of application programming interfaces that allows governments, businesses, start-ups and developers to utilize unique digital infrastructure to solve India's problems of presence-less, paperless, and cashless service delivery. This infrastructure comprises Aadhaar, e-KYC, e-Sign, DigiLocker and UPI. These initiatives are facilitating orderly growth of open banking in India.

Peer-to-peer and marketplace lending: Recognizing the need for an enabling regulatory and supervisory framework to ensure orderly development of the peer-to-peer lending, the RBI has issued "Master Directions" for the Peer to Peer (P2P) Lending Platform in October 2017. All P2P platforms are to be registered as a nonbanking financial company-PSP lending platform, which facilitates participants to lend or borrow. P2P platforms in India can act only as an intermediary providing an online marketplace or platform to the participants while ring fencing its own balance sheet from the funds received from lenders for lending or funds received from borrowers for servicing loans. Nonbanking financial company-PSP lending platforms undertake due diligence on participants and conduct credit assessment and risk profiling of borrowers. They are also permitted to provide assistance in disbursement/repayments/recovery of loans and are required to ensure data localization. However, they cannot raise deposits/lend on their own, nor can they provide or arrange any credit enhancement or credit guarantee. They are also not permitted to facilitate or permit any secured lending linked to its platform, nor cross sell any product except for loan specific insurance products. A total of 21 Nonbanking financial company-PSP lending platforms were registered with RBI as of 31 January 2021.

Equity crowdfunding: Raising funds for companies in India is governed by the provisions of the Companies Act, 2013; the Securities Exchange Board of India Act, 1992; the Securities Contracts (Regulation) Act, 1956; and the Depositories Act, 1996. Equity crowdfunding is illegal.[b]

Cryptoassets: Cryptocurrencies are not currently regulated. However, RBI has cautioned users, holders, and traders of virtual currencies, including Bitcoins, about the potential economic, financial, operational, legal, customer protection, and security-related risks associated in dealing with such virtual currencies. RBI has also clarified that it has not given any license/authorization to any entity/company to operate such schemes or deal with Bitcoin or any virtual currency.

Open APIs: Ministry of Electronics and IT in 2015 notified the Policy on Open Application Programming Interfaces (APIs) for Government of India to promote efficient sharing of data among data owners and inter- and intra-governmental agencies for interoperable systems in order to deliver integrated services. This set of open API is known as the India Stack, which would enable ease of integration of mobile applications with data securely stored and provided by government to authenticated apps. India Stack is a complete set of API for developers and includes the Aadhaar for Authentication, e-KYC documents (safe deposit locker for issue, storage and use of documents), e-Sign (digital signature acceptable under the laws), unified payment interface (for financial transactions), and privacy-protected data sharing within the stack. India Stack enables apps that could open up many opportunities in financial services, health care, and education sectors.[c]

Distributed ledger technology: No dedicated law or regulation governs development, use, and operation of blockchain/distributed ledger technology.

To date, RBI has not initiated any blockchain-based projects. However, RBI supports digital ledger technology and its applications in the financial sector. RBI's Payment System Vision 2019–21 encourages adoption of new technologies for enhancement of digital payment services.

The Inter Regulatory Working Group on FinTech and Digital Banking flagged a few areas for use of blockchain technology in the banking, finance, and the insurance sector, such as centralized KYC, cross-border payments, etc.

The RBI authorized entities to operate the TReDs platform: Mynd Solutions Private Limited, Receivables Exchange of India Limited, and A. TREDS Limited have implemented a blockchain-based solution to check against double financing of the same invoice. Further, the National Payments Corporation of India has designed a distributed-ledger-technology-based system called "Vajra" for automating payment clearing and settlement processes.

The Inter-Ministerial Committee constituted by Government of India is mandated to examine the policy and legal framework for the regulation of digital currencies/virtual currencies/cryptocurrencies and recommends appropriate measures to handle issues. In a February 2019 report it recommended a total ban on private cryptocurrencies through legislation.

Electronic know-your-customer (e-KYC): The Aadhaar e-KYC service of the Unique Identity Development Authority of India enables residents to provide their demographic information to the service provider instantly, digitally, and securely.

Cloud computing: No legislation recognizes cloud computing. Such services would fall under the ambit of Section 43A of the Information Technology (IT) Act 2000. Read with the Information Technology (reasonable security practices and procedures and sensitive personal data or information) Rules 2011, it provides guidelines for collection, use, and protection of, sensitive personal data or information of natural persons by a body corporate that possesses or handles such data.[d]

Artificial intelligence: The RBI in its update to the Master Direction on Know Your Customer in December 2020 encouraged regulated entities to make use of the latest available technology, including artificial intelligence and face-matching technologies to ensure the integrity of the process as well as the information furnished by the customer. However, the responsibility of customer identification shall rest with the regulated entities.

National digital ID enabling financial services: Launched in 2009, Aadhaar is now the largest biometric identification scheme in the world.

Data sharing, privacy, and protection: No comprehensive and dedicated data protection legislation. Provisions of the IT Act, 2000 and the Information Technology (Reasonable Security Practices and Procedures and Sensitive Personal Data or Information) Rules, 2011 framed under it deal with protection of personal information and sensitive personal data and information. The IT Act contemplates the appointment of adjudicating officers to determine whether provisions of the IT Act have been contravened. Implementation on the ground in data protection has been fairly bleak. The government recently presented the Personal Data Protection (PDP) Bill, 2019 in Parliament. It is pending consideration before a joint parliamentary committee. The PDP Bill envisages the constitution of the Data Protection Authority of India (DPAI) for enforcement of its provisions.[e]

Innovation hubs, accelerators, and regulatory sandboxes: In addition to the RBI, the Securities Exchange Board of India and the Insurance Regulatory and Development Authority of India have set up regulatory sandboxes for implementation of innovation. The RBI Regulatory Sandbox creates a platform for testing the viability of proposed products/services without need for a larger and more expensive roll-out. The sandbox aims to foster responsible innovation in financial services, promote efficiency, and benefit consumers. The Securities Exchange Board of India Regulatory Sandbox aims for greater investor participation, people raising capital/providing services, and greater financial inclusion and penetration of financial products, especially in Tier II/III towns and cities.

The RBI in August 2020 announced the setting up of the Reserve Bank Innovation Hub to promote innovation across the financial sector by leveraging technology and fostering innovation. The hub will collaborate with technology innovators and academia. It will focus on promoting access to financial markets and financial inclusion. Its internal infrastructure will promote fintech research and facilitate engagement with innovators and start-ups. While RBI will set the wider objectives for the hub, it do so at arms-length to make way for creative forces.

[a] Cashless India. n.d. Internet Banking. Government of India. http://cashlessindia.gov.in/internet_banking.html
[b] Tax Guru. 2020. Crowdfunding in India. July. https://taxguru.in/
[c] Government of India. 2019. Open API Policy Implementation. Ministry of electronics and Information Technology.
[d] Mani Chengappa and Mathur. 2019. Cloud Computing in India. Lexology. 21 March. https://www.lexology.com/library/detail.aspx?g=e5fe0db7-4a93-4a65-8cfd-0cd36ed6a585
[e] ICLG.com. 2020. India: Data Protection Laws and Regulations 2020.

Japan

Licensing e-money: In May 2019, the Japanese Financial Services Agency issued a report focusing on diversifying payment service providers by lowering entry barriers to the e-money licensing. The key to this report is to ease related regulations so that fintech companies can participate and create new financial services in the e-money market.

Digital banking: Japan's Financial Services Agency established the institutional framework for digital banking in August 2000, and approved the establishment of JAPAN Net Bank, Japan's first internet bank, in September 2000.

Open banking: Starting with the revision of the Banking Act in May 2017, Japan is pushing for open banking. The revised Banking Act, promulgated in June 2017, stipulated that banks should determine and disclose their policies on partnership and cooperation among API companies by March 2018.

Peer-to-peer and marketplace lending: There is no separate regulation for P2P loan lenders, which must be registered as a loan business, and only regulations are applied under the applicable law.

Equity crowdfunding: In May 2014, the Financial Services Agency revised the Financial Instruments Act to promote investment through crowdfunding.

Cryptoassets: In May 2016, Japan's national legislature approved a bill to regulate domestic digital currency exchanges. Moving forward, virtual currency exchange operators will be required to register with the Financial Services Agency. This will implement onsite inspections and administrative orders.

Open application programming interface (API): Under the June 2018 Banking Law Amendment, banks are required to provide APIs to fintech companies.

Distributed ledger technology: The Japanese government enacted the Virtual Currency Act targeting virtual currency exchange operators to protect users and prevent money laundering and financing of terrorism, effective in April 2017.

Electronic know-your-customer (e-KYC): The Japan Financial Services Agency, together with industry associations, established a working group to examine online transactions in June 2017. The working group discussed ways to realize a more efficient digitized onboarding of clients. Based on the results of such discussions, Japanese anti-money laundering laws and regulations were amended in 30 November 2018 to make customer identity verification methods more flexible through electronic methods for non-face-to-face transactions. New KYC procedures that were introduced include: transmission of the picture of the identity confirmation documents (attached with a face photo) and the picture of the customer's appearance; and transmission of the identity confirmation information and the picture of the customer's appearance.[a]

Cloud computing: Establish a project to transform government IT systems into cloud systems (2013).

Artificial intelligence: Japan's Ministry of Economy, Trade and Industry has selected the robot sector as a key strategy for economic growth and announced the robot new strategy for this purpose (January 2015).

National digital ID enabling financial services: In June 2019, the government confirmed its digital ID link to Apple's iPhone. The government has started to develop a standard application for national digital ID.

Data sharing, privacy, and protection: The Personal Information Protection Act was revised in 2015 to protect personal information and pursue development of new industries.

Innovation hubs, accelerators, and regulatory sandboxes: On 6 June 2018, the Regulatory Sandbox was established through the implementation of the Productivity Improvement Special Act.

[a] A. Okada, T. Hori, and T. Iijima. 2020. *The Financial Technology Law Review - Edition 3*. London: Law Business Research.

Republic of Korea

Licensing e-money: Under Article 28, Electronic Financial Transaction Act, to engage in a business issuing and managing electronic currencies will require permission from the Financial Service Commission (FSC). The same will not apply to banks provided for in the Banking Act and other financial institutions prescribed by Presidential Decree. To obtain the permission, it should be a stock company with a capital of at least W5 billion.

Digital banking: The Establishment and Operation of Internet-Only Banks Act was enforced in October 2018. Under it, two internet-only banks were licensed. Capital of an internet-only bank may be at least W25 billion and a nonfinancial investor may hold not more than 34 out of 100 total outstanding voting stock of an internet-only bank.

Open banking: Banks finalized details about their voluntary agreement on the opening banking system in the first quarter of 2019, and the FSC proposed amendments to the Electronic Financial Transaction Act to provide clear legal grounds for the open banking system. The pilot was launched in October 2019 and full operation in December 2019 with 50 institutions (17 banks and 33 fintech firms). More financial institutions and fintech firms will join after completion of the security test.

Peer-to-peer and marketplace lending: In October 2019, the Korean National Assembly approved the Online Investment-Linked Finance and Protection of Users Act. Under it, peer-to-peer (P2P) lending companies must have a minimum of W500 million in capital, while interest rates are capped at 24% a year. The act allows securities brokerage houses, Private Equity Funds, and private lenders to invest in P2P loans.

Equity crowdfunding: Crowdfunding was effective in January 2016 on the basis of amendments to the Enforcement Decree of the Financial Investment Service and Capital Markets Act. To be registered as an intermediary for a crowdfunding offering, a company must have minimum capital of W500 million and meet requirements similar with those of investment advisory services. The amendment increases the limit for an ordinary investor to invest in crowdfunding from W5 million to W10 million per year with an issuer of equity.

Cryptoassets: In late 2016, the government formed the Virtual Currency Task Force, with members from various agencies including the FSC, the National Tax Service, the Korea Fair Trade Commission, the Ministry of Justice, and others. The task force focused on curbing retail investing in cryptocurrencies (via crypto exchanges and initial coin offerings), with no major legal developments in the areas of financial services, securities, or taxation. The Korean National Assembly passed the amendment to the Act on Reporting and Use of Specific Financial Information in March 2020. The new legislation provides a regulatory framework for cryptocurrencies and related service providers. Previously, the government had only issued guidelines, but no actual law was passed. The passing of the amendment signals the official entry of cryptocurrency trading and holding into the legal system for the government. Exchanges, trusts, wallet companies, and initial coin offerings are now required by law to have a real-name verification partnership with an approved Korean bank.

Open application programming interface (API): The Financial Services Commission's open API Framework was launched in December 2019.

Distributed ledger technology: The regulatory sandbox launched by the FSC in April 2019 as the Special Act on Financial Innovation Support includes using blockchain technology.

Electronic know-your-customer (e-KYC): In May 2015, the FSC decided to loosen the strict requirement of face-to-face identification when customers open a new account by allowing alternative methods of non-face-to-face identification. The eased KYC rules facilitated establishment of internet-only banks in Korea in 2018.

Cloud computing: As of October 2018, Korean financial institutions do not use cloud services for their information processing systems, as the Regulation on Supervision of Electronic Financial Transactions only allows the use of a cloud for "non-significant information processing systems" that do not process personal credit data information and unique identification information. However, in January 2019, the FSC eased the relevant regulations to enable the use of cloud services for even "significant information processing systems" by reinforcing the general reporting obligations for financial institutions regarding the use of cloud services and amending the relevant laws to explicitly prescribe their statutory authority to directly supervise and investigate cloud service providers.

Artificial intelligence (AI): The FSC has been leading a joint working group since July 2020 composed of relevant ministries, banks, fintech companies, and AI programming companies to seek ways to improve the current regulations that hamper financial institutions' ability to develop innovative AI-driven products and services. By 2020, the FSC planned to come up with new guidelines on the application of AI technologies in the finance sector and to set up legal norms.

National digital ID enabling financial services: The FSC launched a task force to improve the identity verification system for better financial services. The task force is reviewing various ways to upgrade the existing ID system and actively look into the systems that use the latest verification technologies, such as facial recognition and blockchain technologies. It has been running the regulatory sandbox that allows to test new products and services. There are currently 14 identity verification methods under the financial regulatory sandbox to test.

Data sharing, privacy, and protection: The Personal Information Protection Act was enacted in 2011 as a general statute governing data privacy issues in the Republic of Korea. The FSC and the Financial Supervisory Service of Korea first published their Guidelines on Personal-Information Protection in the Financial Sector in July 2013. The guidelines were intended to provide financial institutions with clear standards on compliance with personal information protection laws, such as the Credit Information Use and Protection Act and the Personal Information Protection Act, and to support them in fulfilling responsibilities for protecting personal (including credit) information.

Innovation hubs, accelerators, and regulatory sandboxes: In September 2018, the National Assembly passed a bill that grants a regulatory sandbox for new businesses in the information and communications technology sector, a development that is expected to speed up adoption and commercialization of next-generation technologies. The bill was to amend the Special Act on Promotion of Information and Communications Technology, Vitalization of Convergence. In May 2020, the FSC published a supplementary fintech regulatory sandbox plan, which includes four new innovative services and a working group proposal on AI in financial services. In particular, the FSC highlighted that its Sandbox Plan supports both financial regulation and financial innovation by allowing fintech companies a period to test their product while it prepares and promotes the direction of regulation. Further, the FSC noted that the new innovative services to the Sandbox Plan include token-based solutions for identity and account verification, as well as virtual financial transactions.

Source: Authors' compilation.

REFERENCES

Alliance for Financial Inclusion (AFI). 2019. Cybersecurity for Financial Inclusion: Framework and Risk Guide. Kuala Lumpur. https://www.afi-global.org/publications/cybersecurity-for-financial-inclusion-framework-risk-guide/.

———. 2020. Creating Enabling Fintech Ecosystems: The Role of Regulators. Kuala Lumpur. https://www.afi-global.org/publications/creating-enabling-fintech-ecosystems-the-role-of-regulators/.

Asian Development Bank (ADB). 2018. Financial Inclusion: New Measurement and Cross-Country Impact Assessment. *Economics Working Paper Series*. No 539. Manila: ADB. https://www.adb.org/sites/default/files/publication/408621/ewp-539-financial-inclusion.pdf.

———. 2019. The Future of Inclusive Finance. Welcome address by Bambang Susantono. ADB Vice-President for Knowledge Management. 6 November. https://www.adb.org/sites/default/files/publication/643831/3rd-asia-finance-forum-conference-proceedings.pdf.

Association of Southeast Asian Nations (ASEAN) Secretariat. 2015. ASEAN Economic Community Blueprint 2025. Jakarta. https://asean.org/book/asean-economic-community-blueprint-2025/.

Auer, Raphael and Rainer Böhme. 2020. The Technology of Retail Central Bank Digital Currency. *BIS Quarterly Review*. March. https://www.bis.org/publ/qtrpdf/r_qt2003.pdf and https://www.bis.org/publ/qtrpdf/r_qt2003.pdf.

Bangko Sentral ng Pilipinas (BSP). 2019. BSP media release. 17 October. https://www.bsp.gov.ph/SitePages/MediaAndResearch/MediaDisp.aspx?ItemId=5076.

Bank for International Settlements (BIS). 2015a. Digital Currencies. Committee on Payments and Market Infrastructures. Basel: BIS. https://www.bis.org/cpmi/publ/d137.pdf.

———. 2015b. Report to BIS Governors Prepared by the Task Force on Data Sharing. Basel. https://www.bis.org/ifc/events/7ifc-tf-report-datasharing.pdf.

———. 2016. Guidance on the Application of the Core Principles for Effective Banking Supervision to the Regulation and Supervision of Institutions Relevant to Financial Inclusion. Basel Committee on Banking Supervision. Basel.

———. 2018. FinTech Credit Markets around the World: Size, Drivers and Policy Issues. *BIS Quarterly Review*. September. https://www.bis.org/publ/qtrpdf/r_qt1809e.htm.

———. 2019a. Embedded Supervision: How to Build Regulation into Blockchain Finance. *BIS Working Paper* No. 811. Basel: BIS. https://www.bis.org/publ/work811.htm.

———. 2019b. The Design of Digital Financial Infrastructure: Lessons from India. *BIS Papers* No. 106. https://www.bis.org/publ/bppdf/bispap106.pdf.

———. 2020. Denis Beau: Stablecoins - a Good or a Bad Solution to Improve Our Payment Systems? Opening address by the First Deputy Governor of the Bank of France, at the Stablecoin Conference—Which Ambitions for Europe?—Organized by Paris Europlace and ConsenSys in Paris. 15 January. https://www.bis.org/review/r200115c.htm.

———. 2020b. Policy Responses to Fintech: A Cross-Country Overview. *FSI Insights on Policy Implementation*. No. 23. Financial Stability Institute.

Basel Committee on Banking Supervision. 2018. Sound Practices: Implications of Fintech Developments for Banks and Bank Supervisors. Bank for International Settlements. https://www.bis.org/bcbs/publ/d431.pdf.

Better Than Cash Alliance. 2017. Building Inclusive Digital Payments Ecosystem: Guidance Note for Governments. https://www.gpfi.org/publications/gpfi-guidance-note-building-inclusive-digital-payments-ecosystems.

Bhunia, Priyankar. 2017. World Banking Report Highlights Role of Agent Banking in Malaysia's Successful Financial Inclusion Push. *Open Gov.* 27 October. https://opengovasia.com/world-bank-report-highlights-role-of-agent-banking-in-malaysias-successful-financial-inclusion-push/.

Business and Human Rights Resource Centre. 2019. Indonesia: Online Loan Sharks Intimidate and Harass Borrowers; Activists Call for Better Regulations. 4 March.

Cambridge Centre for Alternative Finance (CCAF). 2018a. The Second Annual Middle East & Africa Alternative Finance Industry Report. Cambridge: University of Cambridge. https://www.jbs.cam.ac.uk/wp-content/uploads/2020/08/2018-06-ccaf-africa-middle-east-alternative-finance-report.pdf.

———. 2018b. Early Lessons on Regulatory Innovations to Enable Inclusive FinTech. Cambridge, UK. https://www.jbs.cam.ac.uk/wp-content/uploads/2020/08/2019-early-lessons-regulatory-innovations-enable-inclusive-fintech.pdf.

Center for Financial Inclusion. 2019. Handbook on Consumer Protection for Inclusive Finance. Cambridge, MA. https://www.centerforfinancialinclusion.org/handbook-on-consumer-protection-for-inclusive-finance.

Chao, Jerry. 2017. The Gold Rush in Indonesia Payday Loan Market. The Lowdown by Momentum. 2 November. https://thelowdown.momentum.asia/gold-rush-indonesian-payday-loan-market-part-1/.

Committee on Payment and Settlement Systems. 2003. *Policy Issues for Central Banks in Retail Payments.* Basel: Bank for International Settlements. https://www.bis.org/cpmi/publ/d52.pdf.

Digital SME Alliance and European CyberSecurity Organisation. 2017. European Cybersecurity Strategy: Fostering the SME Ecosystem. White paper. Brussels.

Dwoskin, Elizabeth. 2015. Lending Startups Look at Borrowers' Phone Usage to Assess Creditworthiness. *Wall Street Journal.* 30 November. http://www.wsj.com/articles/lending-startups-look-at-borrowers-phone-usage-to-assess-creditworthiness-1448933308.

European Central Bank. n.d. Electronic Money. https://www.ecb.europa.eu/stats/money_credit_banking/electronic_money/html/index.en.html.

European Parliament. 2019. EU Guidelines on Ethics in Artificial Intelligence: Context and Implementation. Briefing. Brussels. https://www.europarl.europa.eu/RegData/etudes/BRIE/2019/640163/EPRS_BRI(2019)640163_EN.pdf.

Financial Services Authority (OJK). 2017. OJK Issues New FinTech Regulation. 10 January. https://www.ojk.go.id/en/berita-dan-kegiatan/info-terkini/Pages/OJK-Issues-New-Fintech-Regulation.aspx.

Financial Stability Board (FSB). Legal Entity Identifier. https://www.fsb.org/work-of-the-fsb/policy-development/additional-policy-areas/legalentityidentifier/.

Finextra. 2019. How to Build the Regulator's Confidence in the Cloud. 12 July. https://www.finextra.com/newsarticle/34114/how-to-build-the-regulators-confidence-in-the-cloud.

G20 Global Policy for Financial Inclusion. 2020. *Promoting Digital and Innovative SME Financing.* Washington, DC: International Bank for Reconstruction and Development/World Bank. https://www.gpfi.org/sites/gpfi/files/saudi_digitalSME.pdf.

Highet, Catherine. 2016. India vs. Pakistan: The Pros and Cons of Two Radically Different Digital ID Systems. *Next Billion.* 10 October. http://nextbillion.net/india-vs-pakistan-the-pros-and-cons-of-two-radically-different-digital-id-systems/.

Global Partnership for Financial Inclusion and G20 Argentina 2018. 2018. G20 Policy Guide. https://www.gpfi.org/publications/g20-policy-guide-digitisation-and-informality-harnessing-digital-financial-inclusion-individuals-and.

Hynes, Casey. Meet Mr. Finance, The Chatbot Schooling Myanmar's Microentrepreneurs in Money. *Forbes.* 8 June 2017.

Ketabchi, Natasha. n.d. Total State of the FinTech Industry (with infographic). *Finance.* https://www.toptal.com/finance/market-research-analysts/FinTech-landscape.

Kim, Sung Su. 2016. Internet-Only Banks to Change the Financial Landscape in Korea and Beyond. *Asian Development Blog.* 31 October. https://blogs.adb.org/blog/internet-only-banks-change-financial-landscape-korea-and-beyond.

IndonesiaGO Digital. 2019. OJK Infinity to Create Friendly FinTech Ecosystem in Indonesia. *Medium Blog.* 9 January. https://medium.com/@indonesiagodigital1/ojk-infinity-to-create-friendly-FinTech-ecosystem-in-indonesia-8f2afa7958b9.

International Finance Corporation (IFC). 2017. Alternative Data: Transforming SME Finance. Washington, DC. https://www.gpfi.org/sites/gpfi/files/documents/GPFI%20Report%20Alternative%20Data%20Transforming%20SME%20Finance.pdf.

International Telecommunication Union (ITU). 2017. Focus Group on Digital Currency including Digital Fiat Currency. http://www.itu.int/en/ITU-T/focusgroups/dfc/Pages/default.aspx.

Kaushik, Preetam. 2019. A Few Bad Apples: How Illegal Lenders Are Abusing Consumers in Indonesia's P2P Sector. *ASEAN Today.* 10 November. https://www.aseantoday.com/2019/11/a-few-bad-apples-how-illegal-lenders-are-abusing-consumers-in-indonesias-p2p-lending-sector/.

Manyika, J., S. Lund, M. Singer, O. White, and C. Berry. 2016. How Digital Finance Could Boost Growth in Emerging Economies. McKinsey Global Institute. 21 September. https://www.mckinsey.com/featured-insights/employment-and-growth/how-digital-finance-could-boost-growth-in-emerging-economies.

McKinsey Global Institute. 2016. Digital Finance for All: Powering Inclusive Growth in Emerging Economies. September. https://www.mckinsey.com/~/media/mckinsey/featured%20insights/Employment%20and%20Growth/How%20digital%20finance%20could%20boost%20growth%20in%20emerging%20economies/MGI-Digital-Finance-For-All-Executive-summary-September-2016.ashx.

Mondato. 2019. Digital Banking in Asia: How to Regulate a Revolution. 8 October. https://blog.mondato.com/regulating-the-revolution/.

Monetary Authority of Singapore. n.d. Principles to Promote Fairness, Ethics, Accountability and Transparency in the Use of AI and Data Analytics in Singapore's Financial Sector. https://www.mas.gov.sg/~/media/MAS/News%20and%20Publications/Monographs%20and%20Information%20Papers/FEAT%20Principles%20Final.pdf.

Nasdaq. 2020. How Cryptocurrencies are Evolving Past the Traditional ICO. 16 March. https://www.nasdaq.com/articles/how-cryptocurrencies-are-evolving-past-the-traditional-ico-2020-03-16.

National Privacy Commission. 2019. National Privacy Commission Conducts Hearings on 48 Online Lending Apps after 400 Harassment Complaints. *National Privacy Commission*. 21 May. https://www.privacy.gov.ph/2019/05/npc-conducts-hearings-on-48-online-lending-apps-after-over-400-harassment-complaints/.

Nilekani, Nandan. 2018. Giving People Control Over Their Data Can Transform Development. *World Bank Blog*. 11 October. https://blogs.worldbank.org/voices/giving-people-control-over-their-data-can-transform-development

Owens, John. 2018. Responsible Digital Credit. Center for Financial Inclusion. https://content.centerforfinancialinclusion.org/wp-content/uploads/sites/2/1970/01/Responsible_Digital_Credit_FINAL_2018.07.18.pdf.

Organisation for Economic Co-operation and Development (OECD). 2019. Task Force on Financial Consumer Protection. Effective Approaches for Financial Consumer Protection in the Digital Age: FCP Principles 1, 2, 3, 4, 6 and 9. http://www.oecd.org/finance/financial-education/Effective-Approaches-FCP-Principles_Digital_Environment.pdf.

Riley, Brian. 2019. Credit Cards and QR Codes: Breakthrough for Financial Inclusion or Too Many Cooks in the Kitchen? *Payment Journal*. August 19. https://www.paymentsjournal.com/credit-cards-and-qr-codes-breakthrough-for-financial-inclusion-or-too-many-cooks-in-the-kitchen/

Swersky, Hadar. 2015. P2P and Balance Sheet Lending: Same but Different... *Finance Magnates*. 28 December. https://www.financemagnates.com/FinTech/bloggers/p2p-and-balance-sheet-lending-same-same-but-different/

Techfunnel. 2020. Digital Banking – The Ultimate Guide. 2 December. https://www.techfunnel.com/fintech/digital-banking-guide/.

United Nations Capital Development Fund (UNCDF). n.d. Financial Inclusion and the SDGs. https://www.uncdf.org/financial-inclusion-and-the-sdgs.

United Nations Secretary-General's Special Advocate for Inclusive Finance for Development. n.d. Briefing on Regulatory Sandboxes. https://www.unsgsa.org/files/1915/3141/8033/Sandbox.pdf.

United Nations (UN) Secretary-General's Special Advocate for Inclusive Finance for Development and Cambridge Centre for Alternative Finance (CCAF). 2019. Early Lessons on Regulatory Innovations to Enable Inclusive FinTech: Innovation Offices, Regulatory Sandboxes, and RegTech. New York and Cambridge. https://www.jbs.cam.ac.uk/wp-content/uploads/2020/08/2019-early-lessons-regulatory-innovations-enable-inclusive-fintech.pdf.

World Bank. n.d. Identification for Development (ID4D). https://id4d.worldbank.org

———. 2017a. Technical Standards for Digital Identity Systems. Washington, DC: World Bank. http://pubdocs.worldbank.org/en/579151515518705630/ID4D-Technical-Standards-for-Digital-Identity.pdf.

———. 2017b. Principles on Identification for Sustainable Development: Toward the Digital Age. Washington, DC. https://documents1.worldbank.org/curated/en/213581486378184357/pdf/Principles-on-Identification-for-Sustainable-Development-Toward-the-Digital-Age.pdf.

———. 2019a. Financial Inclusion Beyond Payments: Policy Considerations for Digital Savings. Technical note. World Bank. Washington, DC. https://documents1.worldbank.org/curated/en/467421555393243557/pdf/Financial-Inclusion-Beyond-Payments-Policy-Considerations-for-Digital-Savings-Technical-Note.pdf.

———. 2019b. Identification, Financial Inclusion and Development in Sub-Saharan Africa. Findex Note. Washington, DC. https://globalfindex.worldbank.org/sites/globalfindex/files/referpdf/FindexNote4_062419.pdf.

World Bank; Cambridge Centre for Alternative Finance. 2019. Regulating Alternative Finance: Results from a Global Regulator Survey. World Bank, Washington, DC. © World Bank. https://openknowledge.worldbank.org/handle/10986/32592.

World Economic Forum (WEF) and Bain & Company. 2018. Trade Tech – A New Age for Trade and Supply Chain Finance. White paper. Geneva. https://www.bain.com/contentassets/83835c319cc649cfa6938dcbeaa7008c/white_paper_trade_tech_report.pdf.

www.ingramcontent.com/pod-product-compliance
Lightning Source LLC
LaVergne TN
LVHW071358070326
832902LV00030B/4646